POCKET GUIDE TO

HOME
MATTERS

POCKET GUIDE TO

HOME MATTERS

CELIA McINNES

StMichael

Illustrations by Mac McIntosh

This edition first published in 1989
exclusively for Marks and Spencer p.l.c.
by arrangement with
the Octopus Publishing Group
Michelin House, 81 Fulham Road
London SW3 6RB

ISBN 0 862735 27 0

Produced by Mandarin Offset

Printed in Hong Kong

CONTENTS

TIPS FOR COOKS

Plan for Success

Organization really is the key to success in the kitchen. Good planning will ensure the smooth and economical running of this aspect of house-keeping, from shopping through to serving up the results to your friends or family. It will prevent those awful moments when your mind goes blank in the middle of the supermarket; you cannot think what to buy for the next meal, cannot even think of a suitable dish that everyone likes, then when you do summon up a recipe suggestion you cannot remember which, if any, of the ingredients you have already at home. So you buy the same old thing you had last week and go home only to find that you did not, after all, have an essential onion, or you buy a lot of different foods at random, then realize that you do not have one whole meal there! So off you go to the (expensive) shop round the corner or to the freezer for yet more convenience foods before anyone demands a meal from you.

You will eat more interesting and varied meals, at less cost and with less effort on your part, if you plan the meals for a whole week at a time. Write down all the main courses and any desserts, then pin up the list somewhere handy in the kitchen so that you can easily refer to it when making up your shopping list.

You do not have to stick rigidly to your 'menu'. It is a guide to help you and you can drop or swap over meals as it suits you.

As well as listing all that you will need for the planned menu of the week, keep an ongoing shopping list of all those many items regularly used in a household as they run out – or are about to run out. Everyone has a different list of 'essentials' that need replacing as soon as they are finished but most households would probably include foods such as sugar, butter or margarine, flour, tea, pasta, rice, peanut butter and stock cubes. A memory board with an attached pen, kept next to the food cupboard or fridge, may be a good idea in families where people do not all eat together at the same time: ask everyone to note down such items as, or – ideally – just before, they finish them.

Work out your menus by going through recipe books to jog your memory as to old favourites you have forgotten, good recipes for that hard-to-get-hold-of ingredient you have just discovered a source for, and new and interesting ideas you might feel up to trying out on this week's visitors.

Arrange the menus so that some of the food needed for the next day can be precooked. For instance, if you are cooking rice to serve hot with curry one day, cook enough to make a rice salad for lunch the following day. If you are making a white sauce to use in a chicken pie, make enough to serve with cauliflower the next day. This sort of planning will cut down considerably on the time spent preparing meals and reduce unintentional leftovers.

COOK AHEAD

Extend the habit of thinking ahead to your cooking. Go in for batch-baking; it will save time and energy (both the sort you pay for and your own). Have a baking morning and make enough cakes, biscuits and pies or crumbles to last a week or two. Freeze the results (or some of them anyway). Even without a freezer, most cakes and biscuits will keep for several days in an airtight tin and desserts for two or three days in the fridge. A session of this sort is also a good way to make use of seasonal gluts of fruit, especially soft fruits which go soft or mouldy very quickly.

If you have a freezer it is well worth cooking double quantities of most dishes and freezing the extras; it is almost as quick to prepare and cook two casseroles as one. Make sure that you put the extra away in a separate container though, or everyone may simply eat twice as much. If you have a child who only eats shepherd's pie or spaghetti or sticks to some other limited regime, set aside several individual portions and freeze them for those occasions when everyone else enjoys curry or chilli for supper.

Minimize the time you spend preparing packed lunches – and add a bit of variety to the usual sandwiches – by cooking something for the lunch box while doing the evening meal.

PLANNING FOR VARIETY

When planning the week's meals, make a point of occasionally introducing something completely new to your repertoire. It is useful to know that the family will finish the meal with no waste when you serve favourite dishes but you do not want meals to become predictable and boring.

Introducing new dishes gradually into the round of old familiars is also a good way of changing the family's diet should you want or need to do this. For instance, you may wish to change to a vegetarian diet or to encourage your children to eat more wholefoods. If you do this little by little, you will have time to experiment with the cooking and the family will have time to get used to the new flavours and textures without any great 'shock of the new'.

Plan menus to take advantage of seasonal foods when they are cheap, plentiful and in prime condition. If you use traditional menus for seasonal foods you will often find that they match the weather conditions too, so warm winter puddings help to keep the cold out while making the best use of autumn apples, plums and pears, for instance. Some seasonal produce can be expensive, but include it when you can afford it: as a treat a plate of strawberries, asparagus or freshly podded peas marks out the year in a very pleasurable way.

Plan meals for variety in colour, texture and taste, as well as for nutritional content. Well-presented food serves to impress the eye and stimulate the appetite – and colour plays an important part in this. If you have a rather neutral main dish, pick vegetables that will brighten up your plate; if it is all green, choose something like tomatoes or red peppers as a contrast. When serving up, mix carrots and peas or sweetcorn and button onions in the same dish, and use garnishes in the same way – parsley on cold meats or kedgeree, paprika on simple mashed potatoes and slivered nuts on almost anything creamy.

A contrast in the texture and type of the different foods presented in one meal also matters. We act on this without thinking when we hand round crisp biscuits with smooth creamy desserts such as fools or mousses or sprinkle crunchy croûtons on to French onion soup. A fresh salad does the same service for a rich pasta dish and yogurt and cucumber raita for a hot curry.

Go for a contrast between courses, too. Try not to use one sort of food more than once in a meal, so serve only one pastry dish; use rice as part of the main dish or for dessert but not both. The same is true for sauces: avoid repeating a sauce similar in taste or texture with both starter and main course, and never serve two or more courses that include cream, or alcohol. It may sound unlikely but it is easy to select separate courses before realizing that they are all rather alike. If you have a rich main course, follow it with something light and refreshing such as lemon soufflé or a fruit sorbet. These are especially welcome to 'clean' the palate after highly spiced main dishes.

A last consideration is the shape and size of the foods making up a meal. Avoid a complete meal made up of small bitty foods, risotto followed by fruit salad, rice pudding after a mince dish, for example. Aim for variety. It really does make the whole meal more satisfying if you balance it in all these ways (it may well be that you do this instinctively anyway).

ENTERTAINING

Entertaining family and friends can be most enjoyable but it does require a little forethought if it is to be successful for all parties – a pleasure for both guests and host or hostess.

Try to pick meals that can be prepared well in advance, with little effort needed at the last minute. One course hot, one course cold and one prepared wholly in advance is a helpful rule of thumb. If your time is limited, it is better to serve simple food well cooked and presented than to attempt a complicated spread that needs a great deal of attention.

Never forget that your guests, however much they appreciate your cooking, actually come to see *you*, and would rather relax with you, talking over a drink, than have you out in the kitchen frantically chopping and basting away. If people are coming for the weekend it is even more important that you plan meals that can be partially prepared in advance and require the minimum of last minute action. Choose simple desserts, such as cheese and fresh fruits or a home-made ice cream or sorbet, that can be served straight from the freezer. Keep main meals filling, with salads and vegetables that are quick and easy to prepare.

If you are going to be out all day, put a casserole or a lasagne in the oven. They can be pre-cooked and reheated (often tasting better for this) or left to cook on an oven auto-timer or, for casseroles, in a slow cooker. An alternative is to leave meat or fish to marinate so that it only requires some finishing touches when you get home. Kebab meat can be left soaking in a spicy sauce and chicken breasts in a marinade of oil and wine or a tandoori paste. Grill them when needed and served with salad and French bread.

If time is really short, make up a large platter of cold foods that can be bought ready to eat from a delicatessen counter or good fishmonger. Serve prawns, dressed crab and smoked salmon with rye bread, pumpernickel and other unusual breads, dark and sweet in contrast to the fish, or a tempting selection of cold meats and pâtés or cheeses, again with good fresh bread.

People's likes and dislikes can be very idiosyncratic, so when someone is invited to dinner, ask if there is anything they cannot bear – most adults will cope discreetly with slight dislikes.

A visitor may have an allergy that you should know about or follow religious dietary laws or, increasingly nowadays it seems, be vegetarian or even vegan (no dairy products either, which can be tricky). Work out a menu that will take all these factors into consideration (plus those discussed earlier on balance and variety) and you will certainly have done something worthy of a pat on the back.

MEALS FOR VISITING CHILDREN

Catering for children successfully is easy, and fun, if you approach it the right way. Children often do not share adults' tastes in food (or drink) so if you have a mixed party it is probably a good idea to serve the children separately.

Fill them up with something reliable that most children like, such as home-made beefburgers, mashed potatoes and beans, or check with the parents in advance that the food you are planning will be acceptable to their offspring.

If you let the children have a first sitting of this sort, they can always return, depending on the goodwill of their respective parents, for titbits from the 'grown-up' spread that follows. At least the parents will be able to relax, knowing the children are not hungry and do not require their attention – anything handed out from their own plate is just an extra treat.

Or give the children a picnic selection of hot and cold finger foods such as tiny rolls of ham, sticks of raw celery, carrot and apple, served each on their own, slices of wholemeal pizza or quiche and fruit-flavoured yogurts. You can actually afford to offer something more interesting if you do it this way as each child can pick out the things he or she likes without any bother. Add jacket potatoes or wholemeal bread as fillers. (This meal can overlap with that for the adults, perhaps adding garlic or herb bread, a dressed salad and some cheeses.

Where food has to be a compromise for a mixed group, such as a fireworks party, the children's needs and tastes really have to be met first or the result will be that no one will enjoy the party. Give the adults 'children's' food rather than the other way round.

If you find that there are more children than chairs, put a plank between two chairs to make a bench on each side of the table, or sit them on the kitchen floor round a tablecloth for a party picnic. If the weather is fine, give them each a tuckbox and send them out into the garden to eat; they will love it.

SHOPPING AND THE STORE CUPBOARD

SHOP AS IT SUITS YOU

When you have a lot to buy it is best to organize a major shop for non-perishable goods – weekly, fortnightly or monthly depending on the cash, transport and storage space available. You can then top this up with occasional forays for fresh fruit and vegetables, bread and fish.

Before you set off, go through the kitchen cupboards and check on what tinned goods, cereals, biscuits and so on you need and how much butter and margarine is left in the freezer, then write a list. It is maddening to stand in the supermarket unable to remember if there were six cans of beans and no cans of tuna in the cupboard, or the other way round. A list need not be followed absolutely, but at least you will get the essentials for the family.

How you shop and how often may also depend on where the shops are in relation to your home or place of work. If you do not have the use of a car, it may well make sense for you to buy from a convenient local shop and pay the slightly higher prices rather than trek across town on the bus. However, it is still likely to be cheaper, as well as easier, to make an occasional trip to a big supermarket and get in a good stock of supplies, even when the cost of a taxi home is added on. Arrange to go with a friend and share the taxi fare between you.

IS IT A BARGAIN?

When you are out shopping it is all too easy to fall for a bargain only to realize later that it was not a bargain at all and may have been a complete waste of money. This can happen just as easily with everyday food shopping as with bigger 'sales' offers.

At the butcher's, for example, you may save a little by choosing a cheap fatty cut rather than a leaner, more tender piece of meat but you then have to take into consideration the greater time and energy that the fatty meat will cost you in terms of preparation and cooking. It may still be a bargain, as long as the family actually *like* the meat. However, if the fat is simply cut off and thrown away you could find that, weight for weight, you have saved nothing. In the same way, it is only worth buying less expensive, own-brand goods at the supermarket if these are acceptable to those who are to consume them.

You can sometimes get some good bargains just before early closing or late on Saturday afternoon, as the prices are slashed on those fresh goods, especially cream, whose sell-by date is nearly upon them. Before you snatch them up, however, check that you will be able to use them up within the two days of the sell-by date recommended by the suppliers. You really do have to use up such items fairly promptly; it is no bargain if the food goes off before you get round to eating it – or, worse, if it gives you food poisoning.

Similarly, before the greengrocer closes for the weekend you can often get fruit and vegetables at a reduced price, when the shopkeeper knows that they are not worth keeping until Monday. Again, think before you buy: you have a bargain only if you have the time to make banana bread with those overripe bananas, soup with all those mushrooms and jam with such a quantity of delicious damsons.

BUYING ABROAD

If you are among the many who now take their holiday abroad, you may already have given in to the urge to bring back a 'taste' of your trip in the form of food or drink. If not, be warned: foods that seem excitingly different when eaten under a foreign sun may not have quite the same flavour when carried home.

If you are interested in canned or bottled foods, remember to allow for their weight (if travelling by air) and their bulk in terms of packing and carrying. It may not be worth lugging along a 10 litre can of olive oil or salted anchovies, however essential these may seem to you as souvenirs. (If you are set on doing it, however, why not do it properly and leave space in the car or take an empty suitcase on the plane with you?)

Of course, people also go on day trips to the Continent, specifically to shop for wine, beer, cheeses, salamis and prettily presented chocolates, conserves and pâtés. They set off by coach or car with full purses and empty bags, typically just before Christmas, and stock up on goods that are either cheaper there, or just different – good as gifts.

When thinking of buying abroad, bear in mind customs regulations. If you fall foul of these you may find yourself out of pocket or with your little treats confiscated. Check before you buy. Alcohol, perfume and tobacco have their own set of rules; read them carefully and if you are not sure if what you have is acceptable, ask. People who are caught in customs often say they thought that they were within the legal limit.

SHOPPING FOR EMERGENCIES

You do not have to live in an isolated farmhouse to be aware of the need for emergency food supplies. Even those of us who live well within walking distance of the shops occasionally cannot make use of them, because of illness in the family, early closing day, or simply lack of time.

It does give you a good feeling to know that you can, nevertheless, put together a square meal from the store cupboard, or perhaps even a special meal. After all it is often when unexpected visitors turn up that you are called upon to provide food at short notice or to extend what you have already, without recourse to the shops.

Get in the habit of stocking up with foods that will form the basis of a meal or that can be used to spread a meal: pasta, canned tomatoes and tuna (and the many other canned foods of course, including soups and vegetables), and rice. Re-stock immediately with such invaluable perishables as onions and garlic, eggs, cheese, bacon, potatoes and bread.

Be imaginative with your short-notice ingredients: instead of thinking 'what do I need to make . . .', think 'what could I make from . . . ?' Mix and match to make the most of what you have rather than fretting over what you don't.

Providing an extra course to the meal – a starter or a salad or a dessert when you had not intended to provide one – is a good way of making the main course go further. Alternatively, make the meal more filling by adding dumplings to the stew, a handful of brown rice to the soup, or a tray of Yorkshire pudding to the roast (a very old way of making meat go a long way).

● Serve a dish of pasta with butter and grated cheese or Parmesan (children like this).

● Make a basic tomato sauce with canned tomatoes and serve it over spaghetti.

● Use canned or frozen vegetables in almost any combination for a salad.

● Mix canned tuna and kidney beans or tuna with cold pasta shells and mayonnaise.

● Home-made soup really does need an onion as its base, otherwise just add what you have: bacon, carrot, celery, pulses, even canned tomatoes or baked beans. Add stock or water and cook.

● For a delicious dessert keep cans of soft fruits in the cupboard to make up a summer pudding or to add to a fruit salad.

With a freezer, of course, you can have an even wider range of foods available – ready-made puff pastry, French bread and pitta bread, for example – as well as complete meals which need only to be de-frozen (if time is short and the casserole solid, stand it in a bowl of tepid water). Things that can be cooked straight from the freezer, such as fish fingers, peas and beans, oven chips and other convenience foods are a further boon to the frantic cook, even if you do not want to use them every day.

FRESH FOODS — WHAT TO LOOK OUT FOR

FRUIT

About 70 per cent of the fruit eaten in this country is imported. It may have been transported some distance and stored or even refrigerated for quite a while, but once it reaches the greengrocers or market stall it ripens then deteriorates fast.

Apricots Make sure that the skin is smooth and free of wrinkles.

Avocado Pinch the narrow end very gently; if it gives slightly it is ready to eat.

Bananas These are ready to eat as soon as they are all-yellow but some people prefer them as they darken; they say that they are sweeter then.

Coconut Shake it to see if it is in good condition; you should be able to hear the fresh milk splashing round inside.

Figs When fresh, these should have a slight bloom to the skin and be slightly soft.

Gooseberries Choose plump, fairly firm gooseberries. The larger they are, the sweeter they are.

Grapes These should be fresh-looking with a bloom on the skins, which should look clear.

Lemons and limes Look for unblemished skins with a slight shine.

Melon A sweet smell is a good sign of a ripe melon, it will also be slightly soft at the end.

Peaches Avoid any with green patches.

Pears It is best to buy these hard and let them ripen in the fruit bowl.

Pineapple A sweet smell indicates that it is ripe. Avoid blackened or soggy leaves.

Rhubarb Buy firm, crisp sticks; the thinner they are, the more tender they will be.

VEGETABLES

Be flexible when shopping for vegetables. Buy what looks good rather than what you have on your list, even if this means altering your plans a little. Vegetables that are to be cooked lightly should be small for the best flavour; larger specimens can be used for long-cooking recipes.

Artichokes These should have green, tightly packed leaves; smaller leaves have more flavour than large.

Asparagus Avoid brown or woody stems and go for green, straight ones. Smaller heads often have a better flavour than plump ones.

Aubergines should be shiny, not dull or wrinkled, and definitely not soft.

Broad beans Pick the smallest you can find; they will be the most tender.

French and runner beans Look for small crisp beans and avoid any that are large and flabby.

Broccoli Look for a firm, dark green head and a crisp stalk; avoid any whose florets are already tinged with yellow.

Brussels sprouts These should be small, tightly curled and bright green.

Cauliflower Avoid discoloured heads; they should be creamy white with tightly packed florets.

Chinese leaves These should have a fresh appearance with tightly packed leaves.

Fennel The bulb should be unblemished and white or pale green. A dark green bulb is more likely to be bitter.

Leeks Small, young leeks have a better flavour; they should be really white with bright green tops.

Okra (ladies' fingers) Do not buy any okra with damaged ridges or brown parts.

Onions Squeeze them if you can, to make sure that they are firm. The skins should be dry and papery.

Parsnips Buy them small, without side shoots; older parsnips have a tough core which reduces the amount of usable vegetable.

Peas Hold the pod up to the light; ideally the peas should be small, with space still left between them.

Peppers These should be firm and unwrinkled, *not* wet.

Spring onions Unless you want them strong, pick small slim ones. The greater the proportion of white, the better.

Spinach Look for bright green, fresh-looking leaves, probably lighter in colour in summer than in winter.

Swedes Very large swedes are difficult to tenderize, so choose smaller ones if possible. Choose roots with whole skins.

Sweetcorn This should be still pale, not yet golden, when you eat it. The leaves should be pale green.

Turnips Choose young turnips, which are green and white, small and round. These have a better flavour than large specimens.

SOME TIPS ON FOOD STORAGE

FRUIT AND VEGETABLES

- Keep apples in a polythene bag in the fridge; put out only a day's supply at a time.
- If you have stored a lemon rather too long and it has dried up, restore its freshness by soaking it in hot water for half an hour.
- Grapes do not improve after harvesting. Keep them cool and eat quickly.
- Do not store fresh figs for more than 24 hours; keep at room temperature.
- Spread out soft fruit on a flat dish so that if one piece goes rotten this does not quickly spread to all the others; it can happen in hours.
- Wrap asparagus in a damp paper towel and keep in a cool place; eat quickly.
- Leave celery in its open plastic bag in the salad drawer of the fridge; this is the best place for it.
- Mushrooms also keep best in their plastic pack or in a sealed plastic container.
- Wrap Iceberg lettuce in a plastic bag and keep in the salad drawer of the refrigerator.

DAIRY PRODUCE

- Surprisingly, skimmed and semi-skimmed milk have a slightly shorter life than full-cream milk — cream seems to act as a deterrent to souring. Always keep in the refrigerator, even in winter.
- Keep all dairy products covered and away from strong-smelling foods.
- Sometimes fruit yogurt pots get bowed tops. This usually means that the yogurt is close to or has passed its sell-by date. The bowing is caused by carbon dioxide produced by the fruit syrup in the yogurt; it is not in itself harmful.
- Keep eggs cool, but not frozen, and stand them with the pointed end down so that the air cell remains floating at the broad end; this delays deterioration.

MEAT AND FISH

- Unwrap meat completely and place on a dish, loosely cover with an open plastic bag (so that the air can still get to it) and put in the coldest part of the refrigerator. When meat is cut up, the risks of contamination are greater, so cook mince and cut-up casserole meat or steak and kidney within the day.

- Before storing a fresh chilled chicken or turkey, remove the giblets and deal with them at once.
- Even 24 hours' storage will leave fish with less flavour and rather flabby. If you have to store it for this length of time, keep it in the fridge with ice cubes on the dish beside it, renewing the ice cubes as they melt. For a longer period, freeze.
- Moisten a side of smoked salmon by brushing with oil, then wrap it closely in cling film or foil and store it in the fridge for up to a week. Interleave slices with cling film or cellophane.

DELICATESSEN

- If you are lucky enough to get a whole salami, hang it somewhere cool and well-ventilated but free from draughts. The fridge is really too cold but if the kitchen is normally above 15°C, 60°F, the fridge it will have to be.
- The more moisture a cheese has, the shorter its life. This is why Cheddar, Leicester and other hard English cheeses keep so well. Wrap in cling film or foil and store somewhere cool. If you do not have a cool larder, use the salad section of the fridge.
- Keep olives covered with light brine in their jar or transfer to a covered container in the refrigerator. A slice of lemon on the surface can help to stop mould forming. Store loose olives in a covered bowl in the refrigerator and run oil through them to restore their gloss.

ORGANIZATION IN THE KITCHEN

GOOD PLANNING

If you want to feel comfortable and to enjoy working in your kitchen, it is important to make sure that it is properly laid out. This does not necessarily mean getting in professional kitchen fitters and spending a lot of money, although increasing numbers of people do seem to buy ready-made kitchens. In fact, just because you have all the 'right' appliances and work surfaces, this does not mean that they have been set out sensibly – all too often things are just popped in where they look nice, or where they will fit most

THE KITCHEN TRIANGLE

The working area of a kitchen has three vital points; a food storage area, sink (plus dishwasher) and food preparation area, and cooker. Ideally, this 'triangle' should be quite tight to avoid too much walking about.

conveniently, regardless of use.

If you cannot rearrange the kitchen cupboards and big equipment, you can usually reorder how you store things and use them. Think carefully before you fill shelves and cupboards and work backwards, i.e. put the most important items in the most accessible places, such as at the front of a low shelf, then less important things behind or above. Rarely used preserving pans, large party plates and things of that sort can go up out of the way on the top of a wall cupboard or at the back of a deep base unit.

Busy cooks often prefer to keep everyday equipment close at hand and leave items such as mixers and processors out on the work surface, ready for use. Put the smaller whisks, spoons, peelers and slicers into a stout pot and stand this at the back of the work surface so that you can reach them easily. Avoid cluttering the work surface too much; keep this sort of thing in a corner where space is not otherwise used. If space is tight, fit wall-mounted scales, a magnetic knife rack and hooks for colanders and sieves. Small shelves fitted on the wall can take herb and spice jars and items often in use, such as the sugar bowl, salt and pepper, and the tea caddy.

All this effort in arranging the kitchen will be wasted, however, if you are not organized in yourself. When you are preparing food work in an orderly fashion, clearing up as you go along. Sort out what is to go in the dishwasher and what you will wash by hand and stack accordingly.

If you come to a natural pause, while waiting for a cake to cool or a jelly to set for instance, take the opportunity to wash up implements and to wipe down the work surfaces.

KITCHEN EQUIPMENT

There is no point in acquiring gadgetry, even of proven versatility, unless you are sure that you will get plenty of use out of it. You may decide to continue using your hand-held grater and balloon whisk; and it would be hard to find more versatile items than a wooden spoon and a sharp vegetable knife.

Good knives are essential in the kitchen: a small paring knife, a large carving knife for meat and a good strong cook's knife for chopping and slicing vegetables and raw meat, should form the basis of a cook's equipment. Choose good-quality carbon steel (easy to sharpen and holds a good fine edge but needs more cleaning after use) or stainless steel.

A selection of wooden spoons and measuring spoons is also endlessly useful (get US measures, too, if you find you have recipes that use these). Saucepans are another essential and today they come in a wide variety of materials from flower-patterned heatproof glass to heavy enamelled iron. Your choice will depend upon the type of cooker you use and your personal preference (and how much you want to pay) but a good middle-priced saucepan is the stainless steel variety with a copper or aluminium base which conducts the heat quickly through the pan; these are hardwearing, nice to use and easy to clean.

Apart from the basics, there are all those specialized items that one cook will feel are essential and another will find completely useless. If your idea of a special lunch is salmon trout or you love sea bass cooked whole, get a fish kettle to cook them in. If you regularly make your own jam and marmalade, splash out on a big stainless steel preserving pan to make the job quicker and easier. On the other hand, if you eat fresh asparagus only once or twice a year, when it is in season, do not clutter up your cupboard with a special asparagus steamer but improvise, using a tall saucepan with a cover for the asparagus heads made from kitchen foil.

Using your imagination to improvise is often essential in the kitchen unless you want and can afford to fill your shelves with rarely used bits and pieces. When you find in the middle of a recipe that a *bain marie* is called for, do not despair: half-fill a deep-sided roasting tin with water and use this instead. Similarly, drop a metal rack or plate inside a saucepan to turn it into a steamer – or even, if it is a pudding, stand it on washed pebbles to keep it out of the water as it steams.

COOK FAST One piece of equipment that has been around for a long time and which cooks either 'never use' or 'wouldn't be without' is the pressure-cooker, which retains its popularity despite the advance of the microwave oven; it makes very quick soups, stews and stock without boiling away all their nutritional content.

COOK SLOW At the other extreme, the slow cooker is the ideal way to cook tough cuts of meat, whole chickens and hams and to make puddings. Its other big advantage is that although it is on for eight to ten hours it uses very little electricity and is safe to leave on unattended.

WORKING IN ADVANCE

Whether the day before you holds a busy round of rushed breakfast, packed lunches and evening meal or one elaborate meal for a special occasion, think ahead and plan out in your mind how and when you are going to do all the little jobs involved in that day's cooking.

Work out which dishes can be prepared or cooked in advance. Instead of saying 'I'll do that later, it only takes a minute', do it now. Many foods can be prepared or part-cooked in advance and some even benefit from this.

Casseroles, for instance, are improved by re-heating; this tenderizes the meat and allows the flavours to blend together. Or you can just start the casserole off: brown the meat and vegetables and place in the casserole dish; add the stock and cook for 30 minutes, then cool and refrigerate until needed. To finish off: place in a hot oven for the first 10 minutes, then reduce to the normal cooking temperature and cook until tender.

Root vegetables, including potatoes, can be peeled several hours before they are needed but they must be completely submerged in cold water, or the exposed parts will discolour. Some people say chips made from soaked potatoes taste better because the starch has been drawn out from them (as, unfortunately, are the vitamins).

Once cooked, long-grain rice can be kept in a covered dish in the fridge for a day or two: to keep out the air as much as possible store in a deep rather than a wide dish and cover with cling film. Use cold for salads or as a base for risottos or stir-fried dishes or reheat by tipping into rapidly boiling water and returning this to the boil for one minute only before draining and serving. Do not do this more than once.

If you want fresh bread rolls for breakfast or for your special meal, make the dough as usual and leave it to rise slowly in the fridge overnight, then bake in the morning. Or, when your dough has risen, shape it into rolls and leave these on a baking tray in the fridge for up to two hours until you need them.

If you are making a quiche, you can partly prepare this ahead of time as well. Line the flan case with pastry and leave to rest in the fridge for two to three hours. Where appropriate, precook the filling and mix the milk, eggs and seasoning in a jug. Store all the ingredients in the fridge until needed: put together and bake.

If you do not want to precook the dish, do as the TV cooks do and weigh out all the ingredients, putting them into bowls and jugs ready for use. Set the oven if necessary and sort out the cooking and serving dishes and prepare them. This not only saves time later, but is helpful if you are following a new recipe.

HOUSEHOLD MAINTENANCE

EMERGENCY KNOWHOW

WHERE ARE THEY WHEN YOU NEED THEM?

We may know where the gas and electricity meters arc but it doesn't occur to most of us to locate the water stopcock or the gas supply turn-off point until we need to do so in a hurry. We should learn where these are *now,* before the emergency arises.

GAS The gas tap is usually near the meter, where the gas supply enters your home, which may be either in the hallway or perhaps in a box on an outside wall.

To turn off the tap, pull the lever so that the notched line on the spindle of the tap lies *across* the tap. (All appliance taps and pilot lights should be turned off first.) To turn on again, return the lever so the notched line lies *along* the pipe. Then relight the pilot lights on all your appliances.

If the lever is too stiff for you to move, do not force it. Call the gas board and ask for someone to come and loosen it – now, *before* you need to be able to turn it off.

WATER Your water supply may have several stopcocks; the more you have, the easier your plumber's job is. He can quickly isolate the affected section without depriving the whole house of water or draining the entire system. The main stopcock may be under the kitchen sink or where the supply enters the house from the street; there will also be a water authority's stop-valve out in the street − from this point on the water supply is *your* responsibility, not theirs.

Check the stopcocks every few months to make sure that they have not seized up.

ELECTRICITY If there is a power cut, the most common electrical 'emergency', turn off fires and cookers in case they are forgotten when power is resumed. Unplug the television and leave on just one light or the radio to signal when the power returns.

Leave fridge and freezer switched on and do not be tempted to open the doors unless you have to: a full freezer, with the door unopened, will re-main unaffected for about eight hours.

Have an emergency kit ready in case the power should fail in the hours of darkness − candles, matches and a good torch. Keep it where you can easily find it in the dark. You may also want to keep a paraffin or calor gas heater for emergen-cies if all your heating is electric.

If the power is only on one circuit in the house and you have re-wirable fuses, keep a packet of fuse wires and a small electrical screwdriver near the main fuse box.

Finally, keep a list of emergency phone num-bers by the phone.

NOTE: When the electricity comes back on, re-member to reset all electric clocks including the clock controlling the central heating.

A BLOCKED DRAIN

If an outside drain or gully is blocked and over-flowing, take out any obvious blockage, such as mud and fallen leaves, then lift off the grid. Using stiff wire (straightened coathanger), an old spoon or your hand in a strong rubber glove, re-move any other debris. Finally, direct a jet of water down the drain to dislodge any remaining blockage and to clean out the drain.

Keep the drain clear by cleaning regularly with hot water, washing soda and a wire brush.

If this does not do the trick and the blockage is too far down the drain to get at, check at the man-hole. If you can work out where the blockage is you may be able to clear it using special drain-cleaning rods which can be hired. Otherwise you will have to call in a professional.

FROZEN AND BURST PIPES

Pipes usually freeze up overnight and the first you know about it is when no water comes out of the tap. Try the various taps and toilets to see if you can work out exactly where the pipe is frozen and to check that it is not also cracked.

If the pipe seems to be undamaged, thaw it out gently using a hair drier or cloths repeatedly wrung out in hot water. Never use a blow-torch: you risk doing further damage to the pipe.

If the pipe has cracked under pressure from the ice (you will know this already if it has thawed and water is pouring everywhere), put a bucket underneath if you can and turn off the water at the stopcock (turn off the central heating too, unless it has a closed separate water supply). You may be able to close off and drain just that section or you may have to turn on all the taps and empty the whole system. Call a plumber.

If you can reach the burst pipe, try an emergency repair. Mix up an epoxy-resin adhesive and spread it on the pipe and on a length of bandage; wind this tightly round the damaged section. Alternatively, wrap it in absorbent cloth soaked in a waterproof glue such as Copydex. As long as the water pressure isn't too high this should hold for a while. There are also proprietary emergency repair kits available, including sticky waterproof tape and a plastic 'putty'.

Unfortunately it is often in the roof space that pipes freeze and burst, because they are not properly insulated. If this causes a flood, switch off the electricity at the mains (to avoid accidental electrocution). Mop up the water and roll back floor coverings. Dry and air as thoroughly as possible – not easy in winter – and do not turn the power back on until you are sure all the water has gone. If the lights fuse, call an electrician.

If a quantity of water is bowing the ceiling beneath and threatening to bring it down, pierce the ceiling in a few places to allow the water to run through; place buckets beneath. Act fast.

A BLOCKED SINK

An important part of every waste outlet is the water-filled trap or U-bend, whose job it is to prevent smells from the main drains from coming up into the house.

If the sink is refusing to empty or is smelling and you think it may be partially blocked, sprinkle a handful of washing soda around the plughole and wash it down with lots of boiling

1. A rubber plunger will usually clear a not too seriously blocked sink. It works best when there is a vacuum, so cover the overflow pipe with a damp cloth.

2. If the sink remains blocked, put a bucket under the U-bend and unscrew it. Old lead pipes have just an opening at the base of the U-bend to unscrew.

water. If this has no effect (do try a couple of times) use a rubber plunger, again repeatedly. Place the cup of the plunger over the plughole and work it up and down. Cover the overflow with a damp cloth and if you have a double sink put in the other plug and cover its overflow too. After the blockage is cleared, clean with soda and hot water.

3. Modern plastic U-bends have either a whole section to remove or a special 'bulb' which comes off quite easily for cleaning.

4. Use a wire to rake out the blockage, or push it through from the plughole. Wash the section before replacing. Flush out with washing soda and hot water.

Everyday Repairs

There are always dozens of little tasks that need doing around the house, where things have broken, worn loose or simply never been quite right. It does not seem worth paying someone to do them, so why not have a go at tackling them yourself? You do not need a lot of equipment, and buying the occasional screwdriver or wrench probably will not even cost the equivalent of one plumber's call-out fee. Nor do you need great skill or expertise, only commonsense.

CHAIR REPAIRS

CHAIR LEGS Wobbly legs on chairs are often caused by the glue in their joints drying out or by screws working loose.

To re-glue, scrape out any dried glue you can see, apply a good woodworking glue to the joints and clamp together to dry. If you cannot fix on a clamp, hold the joints in position by tying a length of strong string round the legs. Tighten this by placing a stick in the string and turning it round several times until the string is really taut. Wedge the stick under the chair seat so that it stays in place until the glue has dried.

If the screws holding the chair together have lost their grip, replace them with slightly larger screws so that they screw in tightly. Dip the screw in wood glue first for good measure.

CANE SEAT To tighten up a sagging cane seat, sponge it top and bottom with hot, soapy water and leave to dry away from heat, if possible out of doors.

DRAWERS THAT STICK

If a drawer annoys you by sticking every time you try to pull it out, wax the runners with an old candle; just rub this hard along the edges.

If this fails to work, chalk the bottom and sides of the drawer and push it back in. When you pull it out again smudging on the chalk will show at which points the drawer is sticking. Rub these down with sandpaper.

A BROKEN LIGHT BULB

Sometimes a light bulb shatters while still in the socket and getting it out without cutting yourself is difficult. Turn off the electricity at the wall or unplug the appliance and insert a cork into the neck of the bulb; you should be able to get enough of a grip on this to unscrew the bulb.

BLEEDING RADIATORS

When you turn on the central heating in the autumn and find that some or all of the radiators are not heating up fully, it is often due to air that has accumulated in the system, preventing the hot water from circulating. Typically the radiator is hot at the bottom, cold at the top.

It is easy to put right if you have a radiator key (available from a hardware shop). Insert the key into the air vent, at one top end of the radiator, and turn gently anticlockwise. You will hear (and possibly smell) the air hissing out; as soon as water begins to bubble out, quickly turn the key clockwise to close tightly (hold a rag close under the key to catch any dirty drips).

CLOSING THE GAP

If there is a gap round the bath or basin or indeed between sink and work surface, shower tray and screen, you worry constantly about the water leaking into the floor or wall there.

Never try to fill these gaps with grouting or ordinary filler; use a silicone rubber sealant which is both waterproof and flexible enough to allow for slight movement. Sealants are available in various colours in tubes like toothpaste. You just trim the end off the nozzle to suit the size of the gap and press the tip into it at an angle of 45°. Keep squeezing and pushing forward steadily so that you feed a bead of sealant along the join. Smooth any unevenness with a wet fingertip or the back of a wetted teaspoon. Try not to mess about with it though – it will become touch-dry within a few minutes.

If the gap is wider than about 3mm (⅛ inches) pack it out first with soft rope or twists of damp newspaper.

REPAIRING BROKEN WINDOWS

Once a window is broken, remove and dispose of the rest of the glass quickly and safely.

1. To remove broken glass from the window frame, hack off the putty, take out the pins holding in the glass and carefully remove it (using pincers for the last two jobs).

2. If the putty is old and has set hard, you may have to chip it out with hammer and chisel. Protect your eyes and hands as you work.

If the glass is only cracked, criss-cross it with sticky tape to hold it firm until you can replace it.

3. Fit the new glass into the frame in a 3mm (⅛ inch) bed of putty and knock in glazing pins parallel to the glass at intervals of about 150mm (6 inches).

4. Finally, press a layer of weathering putty on to the outside, smoothing it to an angle of 45° with a wet putty knife (to throw off rain). After about three weeks paint over the putty and just on to the glass to form a waterproof seal.

TROUBLE WITH TILES

CRACKED CERAMICS A cracked or broken ceramic tile should be replaced, not only because it is unsightly but because, in a wet area, it allows water to seep in.

The difficulty is in getting out the tile without damaging the adjoining tiles. If the tile is only cracked, break it with a hammer or drill into the centre with a masonry bit to get a start. Then lever out the broken pieces with an old chisel or screwdriver; hold adjoining tiles down as you work so that you do not lift them off too.

Clean out the space: tile cement should scrape away quite easily, again with the old chisel blade. If the tile is an old one, set in mortar, you may have to chip it out with a hammer and cold chisel.

To replace, apply tile adhesive to both tile and surface and press in place. Wipe off any surplus adhesive and, when dry, fill the spaces around the tile with grouting. Again, when dry, wipe off the excess with a cloth. (If you are replacing only one or two tiles use Polyfilla to do both jobs.)

TIRED TILING Tiles can become very dirty, not so much the tiles themselves but the grouting in between. Clean tiles with a cream cleanser and a damp cloth. If splash marks show up, rinse with equal parts of vinegar and warm water then wipe dry and buff up.

To clean up grouting that is blackened with mildew, scrub with a weak solution of bleach (see container for strength), using an old toothbrush or nail brush. Protect the bath or basin with newspaper and your hands with rubber gloves. There is also a proprietary product which you can sponge on to old grouting to bring it back to its original bright white or to stain it another colour.

If the grouting is actually crumbling and falling out, rake it out and replace with fresh.

VINYL TILES Vinyl floor tiles are also fairly tough but when they do get damaged they can be tricky to lift. There is no way to get a solvent underneath the tile to release the adhesive, so you will need to use heat.

Lay a square of cooking foil over the tile and press with a hot iron long enough for the heat to penetrate to the underside. You should then be able to prise up a corner of the tile and strip it away. Next remove the remaining adhesive with a heated scraper (the heat softens the adhesive), apply fresh adhesive and drop the new tile into place – be careful not to slide it or you will force the adhesive up between the tiles.

CREAKING STAIRS

A squeaking stair is usually caused by two boards rubbing together. Walk up and down until you track down the exact place then puff in talcum powder or powdered graphite. If you are lucky this will cure the problem. If it does not, or it is more of a creak, it may be that one or more of the triangular blocks that hold the stair risers firm to the treads (the bit you step on) are loose or have come off altogether (there should be two to each step). If you can get under the stairs:

1 Scrape any old adhesive off the block and re-fix with fresh woodworking glue. Avoid putting any weight on that step until the glue has set. If the stairs get heavy wear, provide extra support by screwing on the blocks as well as gluing them.

2 If a block is missing or has split, replace it with metal brackets. Screw these into the angle between tread and riser, making sure that the screws do not reach right through the stairs.

3 If a stair tread is cracked, blocks or brackets will provide good reinforcement if it is not possible to replace it.

4 Look to see if the wedge at the side of the staircase, between the staircase and the tread, is firmly in place. If it is loose, prise it out with a hammer and chisel, clean off any old adhesive, re-glue and knock it back in again. If it is damaged or missing, put in a new one; use a hardwood.

If the underside of the staircase is closed in and you cannot get to it, tackle the problem from above (any carpet will have to come up).

5 Lever up the offending tread with a nail bar or hammer and cold chisel – only very slightly, enough to squeeze in some wood glue. Release and, for good measure, screw down into the front edge of the tread (where it meets the riser) with two or three countersunk screws.

TO REPAIR A DRIPPING TAP

Turn off the water supply to the tap. Unscrew and lift up the cover to reveal a hexagonal nut; holding the spout, undo the nut with a spanner.

Lift the top of the ta away from the body. At the lower end is a spindle (the jumper); the

SHROUDED HEAD TAP

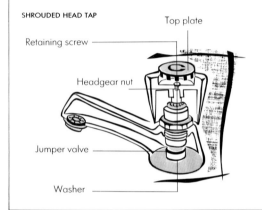

Top plate

Retaining screw

Headgear nut

Jumper valve

Washer

A DRIPPING TAP

Constant dripping can result in a build-up of scale on the bath or basin beneath and also lead to a frozen waste pipe if it is left to drip right through a freezing night. The usual cause is a worn washer inside the tap which should be replaced with a new one of exactly the same size.

Some modern taps have a head that just pulls off, or comes off once you have undone a small retaining screw on the head. This may be concealed under the hot or cold indicator on the tap, which you just prise off.

PROBLEM FLOORBOARDS

SQUEAKING FLOORBOARDS Talcum powder or perhaps French chalk may be the answer where boards are rubbing against one another.

Sometimes boards creak because they are not properly nailed down. Nails may be missing or loose or too small; check and see. When you renail be sure to nail only into the joists – use the

washer is held on to this with a small nut.

Undo the nut and remove the washer; replace with a new one. Reassemble the tap, working in reverse order. Leaving the tap half on (to avoid airlocks), restore the water supply.

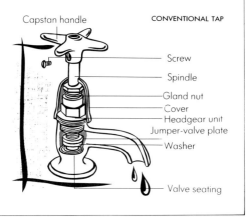

Capstan handle

CONVENTIONAL TAP

Screw
Spindle
Gland nut
Cover
Headgear unit
Jumper-valve plate
Washer

Valve seating

previous nail line as a guide.

GAPS BETWEEN THE FLOORBOARDS For a neater appearance and fewer draughts, fill small gaps with wood filler or *papier mâché* made from newspaper soaked and mixed with glue size or wallpaper paste.

For larger gaps, use wood strips tapered on one side. Apply woodworking glue to each side and tap the strip down into the gap. Plane level once the adhesive has set.

A STICKING DOOR

To find out where the door is sticking, slip carbon paper between door and frame, then close the door. If the carbon marks the bottom corner of the door, take it off its hinges (not difficult if it is on rising-butts) and shave the corner down with a plane or Surform. Replace.

If the top corner sticks it may be because the door has dropped with age. If the hinges look worn and slack, fit new ones or swap the top and bottom hinges round to even out wear on them.

Sometimes a door begins to rub purely because of the number of layers of paint on it. Remove some with a Surform or some paint stripper, rub down with sandpaper, prime and repaint.

HINGES that are stiff or noisy may need no more than a drop of lubricating oil to cure them.

EXTERIOR UPKEEP

Wear and tear on the outside of the house tends to be gradual and often goes unnoticed until it presents itself as a major, and a costly, problem. Get into the habit of systematically inspecting the house, to make sure it is as weatherproof as you can make it. Begin at the top and work down.

● Check the roof for loose or broken tiles.

● Look at the mortar round ridge tiles, eaves and chimney pots to make sure that it has not cracked or been pecked away by birds in search of a nesting place.

● Check that roof flashings are sound.

● If there is a problem, you will probably want to call on professional help for these jobs, if only because they mean working at a height. For your tour of inspection use a pair of good binoculars if you are unhappy about ladder work; this is what estate agents and surveyors do.

● Inspect all the exterior woodwork. Scrape off flaking paintwork, prime and repaint. (Oil bare timber sills and thresholds.)

● Check the rendering for cracks and bare patches: small faults can be filled in with a thin paste of mortar but where a large patch has come loose ('blown') you should hack the whole section back before re-rendering.

● Where the pointing is crumbling away between the bricks, rake this out with a hammer and cold chisel and replace with fresh mortar.

● Is the brickwork sound? Scrape any mould or algae off exterior walls then wash down with a solution of half bleach, half water. Leave to dry then repeat the next day. If the mould persists, look for the source of the damp that is causing it.

- Make sure that airbricks at or below ground level have not become clogged up. Sweep away any dirt and clean out the holes in the airbrick. It is important that airbricks are kept clear, as they provide essential ventilation for wood floors.
- Never pile earth up against the outside walls of the house so that it comes above the line of the damp proof course. This will serve as a bridge for damp to pass from the ground up into the brickwork – and from there into the internal plastering as well.

WINDOWS AND DOORS

- Wood tends to shrink with age, leaving gaps between the frame and the adjoining masonry. This will allow water to seep in, especially during driving rain.

Seal all gaps in the frames with mastic from a tube or cartridge and paint over once its surface has hardened – it will only take a few days. Do not use a cement mortar or putty as both will harden and cracks will open again.

- Never ignore damaged putty in frames; it lets in damp which, over time, causes rot in timber and rust in metal. Remove the putty (badly weathered putty falls off in strips) and replace with fresh. Paint over when dry.

If sections of a wooden window frame have become damp, wait until they dry out: if the wood is hard but cracked, fill with a fine surface filler, rub down, prime and repaint; if it has become soft (try with your thumbnail or a key), cut back until you reach sound wood, then insert a new section, gluing it with a waterproof product. Fill gaps, smooth, prime and repaint.

- Repair cracked or rotten window sills. Check that the drip groove on the underside of the sill is clear; if it is blocked, rain will run across straight into the wall.
- Doors are particularly vulnerable at the base, both from rising damp and from driving rain forcing water underneath. Replace if rotten and try to resolve the cause of the damp. If driving rain is the problem, fit a weatherboard across the bottom. (If you already have one but it is not functioning properly, replace it.)

GUTTERING AND DOWNPIPES

These will not do their job properly if they are either blocked or faulty – if, for instance, they either overflow or leak at the joints. The best time to check on this is when it is actually raining; when the rain stops you can get to work.

BLOCKAGES Clear out the gutter; remove any mud, leaves or tile sediment with a trowel, working from the downpipe outlet towards the stop end so that the debris is not pushed down the pipe. Then pour in water from the stop end to wash away the remains (put a bowl under the outlet so this does not go straight down and block the drain). If the downpipe is also blocked, use a length of strong cane or wire to dislodge the blockage (drain-cleaning wire is good if the blockage is well down the pipe). Again, catch any debris.

To help prevent further trouble, stretch a strip of chicken wire over the gutter to keep out leaves and bird's nests – this may be a good idea for chimney pots, too.

LEAKING JOINTS If your rainy day check did not show it up before, the bucket of water will reveal any faulty joints. These matter because they allow rainwater to drip against the brickwork and eventually penetrate it. Dark patches or green algae on the wall are a sign that this is happening.

On old metal pipework, seal the weak joint with a non-setting mastic or self-adhesive metal flashing strip. On plastic pipework, the connecting part may not be clipped in fully, or it may need a new sealing gasket.

SAGGING RUNS Finally, overflowing may be caused by sagging guttering. To confirm this look to see if any water from your bucketful remains in a dip in it. Check that all the brackets supporting the gutter are firm, that their fixings have not worked loose and that the fascia board to which these are attached is not damaged or rotten. Replace as necessary.

As the old cast-iron guttering is heavy to work with and needs regular maintenance by way of rust proofing and painting, it may be worthwhile replacing it with plastic.

DAMP

Despite all the advances in building technique and the higher standards of comfort we demand today, simple damp – rain, moisture – does serious damage to the fabric of the home. It should always be taken seriously: it ruins your wallpaper and stains the walls, crumbles off plaster, blackens windowsills and rots timbers.

Wherever damp is suspected the rule should be to deal with it as soon as possible, for the longer it is left the more serious will be the problems of repair. The job that would have prevented the damp occurring in the first place may have been as simple as clearing out a gutter at the top of the house or an airbrick at ground level (see p. 41).

It is not always easy, however, to work out the source of a damp patch. There may even be more than one cause or one form of damp may obscure another. The three main sources are:

- rain penetration
- moisture rising from the soil (rising damp)
- moisture-laden air leading to condensation.

Where you are having trouble with damp there is one simple test you can perform. Tape a piece of kitchen foil on to the affected wall or floor so that all the edges are sealed by the tape. If after a couple of days there are drops of moisture on the outside of the foil, your problem is condensation; if the moisture is on the inside, the problem is damp (rising or penetrating). Carry out this test on any solid floor to check if it is dampproof before you lay down new flooring, which could be ruined if damp is rising through the floor.)

CONDENSATION

Condensation can cause both structural and surface damage in the home. Air always contains water vapour which is taken up as it heats; if the temperature drops or the air comes into contact with a cold surface, the water condenses, that is, it returns to liquid form. The warmer the air, the more water it can hold as vapour. In a warm house the problem of damp from condensation can sometimes be worse than in a cool one, once the air either reaches saturation point or meets with something cold such as a window, mirror or exterior wall. There is simply *more* water vapour *to* condense and you can actually watch it happening – water droplets running down the window after you have had a bath perhaps.

At least on the window it is possible to wipe up condensation, though it does seep into the frames where it encourages black mildew to grow and rot to develop. But high up on a wall or behind a cupboard the dampness will sink into the plaster.

Also, it is often in the well cared-for, insulated, double-glazed home that condensation does become a real worry because there is no escape route for the damp air. Keeping a good balance between heating and ventilation is the key to preventing damp through condensation.

WHAT YOU CAN DO

- Avoid using paraffin heaters and unflued gas or oil heaters.
- Keep cooking pans covered.
- Instal an extractor fan – as high as possible – in the kitchen and bathroom, placing it opposite the door if you can.
- Fit a cooker hood to remove steam.
- Run cold water into the bath before hot.
- Use the outlet tube of the tumble dryer out of the window.
- Never block the air vents let into closed-off fireplaces.
- Use special anti-condensation paint in vulnerable rooms.
- To warm window surfaces, fit double glazing.
- To warm walls and ceilings, line with expanded polystyrene sheeting under wallpaper or with cork tiles.
- Generally increase the ventilation in the house, opening windows at least once a day.

Where you have a problem, wash the wall down with a solution of bleach and water (see container for strength) or with a fungicide, but remember that these only get rid of fungus, not the cause of it. Fungicidal paints and wallpaper adhesives are also available.

PENETRATING DAMP

With penetrating damp you are seeing the effects internally of the sort of problems covered earlier (see Exterior Upkeep, pages 40-2) – tiles missing, cracked rendering, faulty weatherboards as well as others, such as porous brickwork. If your home is well maintained and is kept in good order you should not have any trouble with penetrating damp.

These problems become apparent particularly during spells of wet weather (though their effects may linger on). Go into the roof space and check the roof: look for tell-tale rivulets down rafters, wet patches on the floor or down the chimney breast. Wherever you have signs of damp look to see if they get worse with rain and try to work out why this might be. Go outside – is the gutter gushing over just above the spot where your bedroom ceiling is stained? Can you see loose flashing to the bay roof over the lounge window where your new wallpaper is peeling off? The damp may sometimes appear some distance from its source; rain may run down joists or roof timbers for several metres before it drips down into the room below and where it is blown by driving winds it may again travel some distance before showing itself.

Efflorescence on plaster or brickwork can be a sign of porous brickwork. (It does also occur as new plaster dries out.) Efflorescence is the name given to an accumulation of salts in a wall which crystallize on the surface to form a powdery white deposit. Clean off the salts with a dry brush (do not wash) and treat the wall with a waterproof rendering (inside) and/or a silicone waterproofing fluid (outside or inside).

Other signs of old, porous bricks and perhaps crumbling mortar between them are persistent damp patches in the *middle* of external walls, appearing especially after rain, and possibly algae growing on the outside.

Penetrating damp is really more a problem of older homes with solid walls. In modern houses built with cavity walls, some or all of the rain coming in is likely just to run down inside the outer layer of bricks.

RISING DAMP

This is potentially the most difficult and expensive to deal with. It is caused by water being drawn up from the ground into the floors and walls of the house by natural capillary action. This will happen unless there is a waterproof barrier to prevent it.

WALLS Modern homes are built with a damp-proof course (known as a dpc) in the walls; it may show as a black line between two courses of bricks. Older properties have usually had a dpc inserted, or injected in the case of a silicone-based liquid dpc, and trouble arises when it fails or is bridged in some way. Wallpaper peels off at the bottom and a damp tidemark may show above the skirting, getting higher after wet weather. Worse, where you cannot see what is going on, joists and floorboards quickly become affected by wet and/or dry rot.

If you have no dpc (we are talking about ground floor or basement properties only here), get quotes from well-established specialists and have one installed. If you have a dpc, check to make sure that none of the following has occurred – all are common things that bridge a dpc enabling moisture to bypass the waterproof barrier.

• Earth piled up against the outside wall above the level of the dpc.
• Paving laid above the level of the dpc.
• Rendering carried down past the dpc on the outside or plaster carried down past it inside.
• If the dpc is not high enough above ground level heavy rain will splash above the dpc. It should be 150mm (6in).

FLOORS A wood floor is not usually a problem but any solid floor, where the concrete is actually sitting on the ground, will draw up moisture and transmit it through into whatever flooring is laid over it – often lifting and ruining it.

A solid floor should be laid over a dampproof membrane of heavy-duty polythene which should link up with the dpc in the walls. If this has not been done, all you can do to avoid taking up the whole floor is try to seal it with a polyurethane or bitumen-rubber based sealant.

UNWANTED SMELLS

IN THE KITCHEN

Just a little forethought will stop cooking smells:

• If you are cooking something with a smell that you would not want to travel all over the house, work with a saucer of vinegar beside you; it will absorb most of the smell.

• When cooking cabbage, put a few drops of fresh lemon juice in the water; it will stop the smell spreading without affecting the taste.

• Add celery to the cooking oil when you fry fish; it will help to disguise the smell.

• Chopping boards tend to absorb the smell of foods and washing does not always remove it. Rub a paste of bicarbonate of soda into the board, rinse, then wash as usual. To get rid of the smell of onion, rub over with coarse salt before rinsing with cold water.

• If silver cutlery has a fishy smell clinging to it, add a drop of mustard to the washing-up water. A little vinegar added to the water will remove fish smells from china.

• Refresh a clean saucepan that has a lingering smell by boiling a little white vinegar in it.

• Wash oniony or garlicky smelling hands as soon as possible with *cold* water; if the smell persists, rub with lemon juice or vinegar and wash with soap and water.

• Clear the fridge of lingering odours by smearing a paste of baking soda around the inside. Or use one of the following to absorb them: charcoal, baking soda or simply crumpled-up newspaper. If none of these does the trick, turn the fridge off, then wipe it out with a solution of the sterilizing fluid used for babies' bottles (*not* on the metal parts). Rinse the inside and leave to dry before turning it on again.

AROUND THE HOUSE

• The smell of fresh paint very quickly palls. Remove it by leaving a small dish of kitchen salt in a newly painted room overnight.

• Very strong chemical smells can be removed by using a peeled onion in a bucket of water.

IN THE DUSTBIN

● Keeping a mothball in the bottom of a dustbin improves its smell and keeps away flies.

AFTER ENTERTAINING

The worst culprit is cigarette smoke:

● Place a small bowl of vinegar in the room where people are smoking to absorb the smell of the smoke. You can also buy special candles which do this job as they burn; just light one and place it on the table or mantelpiece.

● When your guests have gone out of the door, get rid of lingering smoke by whisking a damp towel round the room. If the smell persists, dilute a few drops of ammonia in water and leave this in the room overnight.

Garlic breath comes a close second:

● For a really effective remedy, forget peppermints – chew fresh parsley or a coffee bean.

CUPBOARDS AND DRAWERS

● If a little-used cupboard has become rather musty, put a saucer of bath salts on the floor.

● For drawers that have not been aired, pop in lemon peel or small pads of cotton wool with a little vanilla essence. To keep a drawer smelling sweet, use perfumed drawer liners.

ACCIDENTS

● If the cat or dog is sick on the carpet just before visitors arrive, a quick squirt from the soda syphon will help to eliminate the smell once you have cleared up.

PLEASANT SMELLS

Make the house smell fresh and welcoming with bowls of *pot pourri* or dried lavender; for a cosy evening at home burn incense sticks or perfumed candles (be careful not to overdo it) and put orange or lemon peel on the open fire.

Finally, it is said that you can add several thousand pounds to the price of your home if you welcome potential buyers with evocative smells like: fresh coffee or just a few beans roasted in the oven, fresh herbs, such as rosemary, cooked under the grill, a warm loaf of bread in the oven.

SOME HOME-MADE CLEANERS

It does seem that these days one can buy a proprietary product to deal with almost any cleaning job. However you may not have what you need to hand at the right moment, and besides, these jars and aerosols can be expensive. Try these home-made tips and solutions and save time and money.

OVENS Ammonia makes an inexpensive oven cleaner but it can burn the skin, so wear rubber gloves, handle with care – and watch your eyes. Where food is burned on to the bottom of the oven, leave this to cool then sprinkle on dishwasher powder. Cover with a damp paper towel and leave overnight; wash off with warm water the next day.

METAL AND CHINA Scouring with wood ash will take some stains off china and metal objects.

MARBLE Make your marble table-top or fireplace surround shine by rubbing with a slice of lemon, wrapped in a clean cloth and dipped in borax.

WINDOWS For a good window cleaner, dilute cold wash detergent: 1 capful to 1 litre (2 pints) of cold water. Polish up afterwards with crumpled newspaper.

CHROME AND PAINTWORK Polish with a mixture of 2 parts paraffin to 1 part methylated spirit.

FURNITURE POLISH To remove the grime of years and bring a shine to a piece of old wood furniture, clean with one of the following combinations:

- 2 parts linseed oil to 1 part of turpentine and 1 part of water.
- Equal parts of raw linseed oil, turpentine and methylated spirit.

Mix in a glass screw-topped jar and shake well; apply with a soft cloth pad, replacing this as it gets dirty. Once cleaned, polish up with a good wax polish.

UPHOLSTERY A mixture of 1 part detergent to 4 parts boiling water will cool to a jelly. Whip it up with an egg beater and use the resulting foam to clean upholstery; it works. Another good emergency cleaner for upholstery is the sort of shaving cream that comes in an aerosol can.

DOWN THE DRAIN Make a solution of 15 ml (1 tablespoon) salt to 600 ml (1 pint) hot water to clear the drain and get rid of any nasty smells.

WALLS To wash down dirty walls, combine ¼ cup washing soda, ½ cup ammonia and ¼ cup white vinegar in a bucket of warm water.

FLOORS For sparkling linoleum or PVC tiled floors, rinse with a bucket of water to which 1 cup of white vinegar has been added.

PAINTING AND WALLPAPERING

PREPARATION

However many coats of paint you apply and however pretty and subtle the colour, you will be wasting your time if you have not prepared the surface properly in advance.

- It must be clean and dry or the paint will not take. Wash, especially woodwork, with sugar soap and water, working from the bottom up to avoid dirty streaks.
- It must be sound. If old paint or paper flakes off as or after you work it will take your paint with it. So brush and scrape off any loose material and fill cracks or holes with the appropriate grade of filler.
- If the wall surface is pitted and uneven (but otherwise sound) consider covering it with lining paper before overpainting.
- Rub down woodwork with sandpaper to give the new gloss a rough surface to grip on and to get rid of any build-up of old paint or run marks.
- Old wallpaper *must* come off unless it is just the one layer, still firmly attached, clean and fairly inoffensive in colour and pattern.
- If you are working on new plaster or plasterboard, seal it first with a primer (but not before plaster has dried out, which may take several weeks); never paper newly plastered walls.
- Deal with any damp or other problems before you set to work. Do not imagine that the stain will just disappear; it will soon be back.

PAINTING TIPS

When you begin a painting job you need a clear run at it. Remove any fittings that will get in the way (turn off the electricity at the mains first for light fittings and seal wires before turning it back on). Take down curtains and cover any furniture that has to stay in the room with a dust sheet. If you cannot take up carpets, cover with sheeting and protect the edges with masking tape.

- To avoid dust spoiling the effect of your new gloss paint, vacuum before you begin to paint and wipe over horizontal surfaces with a cloth dampened with white spirit. Wear cotton rather than wool work clothes.

- Always wipe the top of the paint tin before you open it to avoid dust falling in. Cut round the edge of any skin with a knife and remove it; do not try to stir it in. If necessary, strain out any bits or lumps through old nylon tights.

- Use the right brush for the job; they come in a variety of sizes and you can get special angled ones for window frames and behind radiators. Use a roller for large areas, doing the edges first with a brush.

- Decant a small amount of paint into a paint kettle to avoid carrying a heavy tin, with the risk of spillage and wastage.

- Work in the correct order: ceiling first, walls, then woodwork (in the following order: picture rails, skirtings, windows, doors). If you are papering the walls, do this last.

- If you are worried about drips while working on the ceiling, try using a 'solid' emulsion.

- Apply paint in vertical strokes then spread it at right angles to even out the coverage. Emulsion paint should not show brush marks when it dries but finish off gloss with light upward strokes for the best result.

- Keep a cloth moistened with a little white spirit to hand to mop up odd drips and spills.

- Never try to hurry a job by applying one thick coat; two thinner ones will give a smoother finish and will wear better. And remember that if you buy cheap paint, you will often end up having to do four coats instead of two to get a decent coverage.

- Finally, when you have finished, for the day or for good, clean brushes or rollers promptly.

WALLPAPERING TIPS

To estimate how many rolls you need measure the height of the room and work out how many lengths you can cut from each roll (remember to allow for pattern matching). Multiply the number of lengths by the width of the paper and divide this figure into the total perimeter of the room: when estimating, do not allow for doors or windows (unless these really are enormous). Buy enough paper to finish the whole job. Look at all the rolls before you start and shuffle to get a mix if there is any slight difference in shade. Now you are ready to go.

● Apply a coat of size (watered down adhesive) to the wall to seal it and to give a smooth surface on which to slide the paper into position.

● Cover badly blemished walls with lining paper applied horizontally, then hang your chosen paper vertically.

● Begin work by the window (mistakes will not show up so much there) except when your paper has a large pattern, in which case begin so that this hangs centrally at any special feature such as a chimney breast, then work round the room in both directions.

● Most wallpaper pastes take 15 to 20 minutes to thicken so prepare in advance. Tie a string across your paste bucket to balance the brush on when it is not in use and to remove excess paste from the brush when it is.

● Start by marking a true vertical line and hang to this: hang a plumb line and mark along it or chalk the line and snap it against the wall to mark a line. Work from a *new* vertical every time you start again, for example, after a corner.

● Do not use a seam roller on embossed papers as it will flatten the raised surface. Tap the edge gently with your brush instead.

● If a blister in the paper does not disappear naturally, puncture it and brush flat or, if it is large, cut a cross over it with a knife then repaste the flaps.

● For a neat effect round fiddly fittings such as switches and sockets, unscrew and loosen the front a little so that you can tuck the paper underneath, then refix. Turn the electricity off while you do this for safety's sake and never do this with any metallic wallcovering.

SAFETY

- Use a steady stepladder, of such a height that you do not have to stand on the top rungs but can support yourself on it if necessary. For ceilings and awkward areas, such as stairwells, rig up a secure ladder and trestle system.
- Wear sensible clothes, with no trailing sleeves or ties that may catch, or old slip-on shoes that could easily slip *off* at a vital moment.
- Take precautions to protect yourself: goggles and face mask for sanding or chipping away at something; rubber gloves for handling paint stripper and other strong chemicals. Should paint splash in your eye wash it out at once with water. Never smoke while painting.
- Children are involved in one-third of DIY accidents. Keep them out of the way – and never leave paint thinners, varnishes and so on where they could get hold of them.

FIXING GUIDE FOR BEGINNERS

USING NAILS AND SCREWS

Nailing and screwing are not interchangeable; they do in fact have different strengths and, on the whole, different applications.

Big coarse nails are used for rough work such as fixing down floorboards while finer panel pins are used for woodwork where the appearance matters or to hold together two pieces of wood while an adhesive is setting. There is a huge variety of nails, including masonry nails for fixing skirtings or battening to brickwork, galvanized nails for roofing felt, hardboard pins and brass chair nails for upholstery work. They are sized by length; the gauge or thickness will be appropriate to this or may be differentiated, e.g. fine, medium.

Having picked the right nail, begin by steadying your work on a firm surface, then tap the head gently. Try to hit it square so that it goes in straight (when you are more experienced you can insert nails at a slight angle for extra strength).

After a few taps put a bit more force into it. To remove nails, use pincers or a claw hammer.

Screws also come in different sizes and gauges but fewer varieties, although there are special screws for chipboard and screws with chromed caps for fixing mirrors. The main distinctions are between round-headed and countersunk screws (the former for fixing metal to wood, the latter flat to fit flush with the surface it goes into); and between those with the traditional cross-head slot and those with the Posidriv cross-slotted head.

The holding power of screws does not depend on the force used to drive them in; the secret is to start holes into which the screws can be driven with the minimum of force. Begin by making a starting hole with a bradawl and help it to go in by dipping the tip in grease or wax (this also discourages rust).

If you are drilling a hole for the screw this should be slightly smaller than the maximum diameter of the screw thread. If screwing into a wall, drill the hole and fill with a wallplug first; hole, plug and screw must be related in both width and length.

Although nailing is quicker, screwing is stronger and screws are easier to get out at a later date, should this be necessary. To remove stiff or rusty screws apply a loosening oil or try to tighten the screw to break its hold or tap it with hammer and screwdriver, then see if it will turn.

DRILLING FOR THE NOVICE

Drills can be used to make holes in a variety of materials – wood, metal, brick and even plastic. A hand drill is slow but easy to control and can be used on wood and metal while a hand brace is good for drilling large diameter holes in wood.

For drilling into masonry, however, you really need a power (electric) drill. These are fast and very versatile; with the correct drill bit, they will make a hole in almost anything. For general use, buy a two-speed or variable-speed drill of 350 to 500 watt power with hammer or rotary action.

DRILL BITS These are the detachable parts that actually bore the holes and you change the bit according to the job you are doing. Drill bits come in different sizes and materials, for instance carbon steel twists for wood, high speed steel twists for metal and tungsten carbide-tipped for masonry; ask for advice until you learn by experience which to choose.

Drill bits also come in very different qualities; always go for good quality here, even though it means more expense to start with. Cheap bits will break and go blunt far more readily; they are not worth the initial saving.

CHUCK KEY The bits fit into the drill chuck which you open and close with the chuck key. Always make sure that the bit is securely held in the chuck or it may come out and get stuck in the hole you are boring: put it right in and tighten the key really firmly.

USING THE DRILL It is important that you use the drill correctly. Hold it steadily at right angles to the job and do not let it waver. Maintain an even, steady pressure if you want a neat hole. Be careful not to move the bit out of position while you are drilling; this will spoil the hole and may break the bit if you are using an electric drill. Apart from being irritating, this can be dangerous.

To stop, with a hand drill just drill in reverse; with an electric drill continue the power and at the same time draw the bit (straight) out of the hole.

When drilling into something slippery or something that may crumble (tiling, for example), first tape over where you want to drill.

To ensure that you drill just to the right depth, mark this on the drill bit, again with sticky tape.

SAFETY NOTE

Never leave a power drill lying about, plugged in, where a small child may be tempted to pick it up and pull the trigger.

ADHESIVES

You can stick almost any one material to any other satisfactorily as long as you choose the right adhesive. Most adhesives are easier to apply and set faster in warm conditions and they will not work properly on dirty or greasy surfaces or where the two surfaces do not fit closely.

CONTACT ADHESIVES Useful with wood and hardboard, metal, hard plaster and rubber (not vinyl) flooring and rigid plastics (e.g. Formica), contact adhesives work as soon as the two surfaces touch. Spread the contact adhesive thinly on both surfaces and leave to dry for a while (see makers' instructions). With the exception of the thixotropic sort, you cannot move the two pieces at all once they have come into contact with each other.

For safety, pick a non-flammable type; any spills can be cleaned up with water.

CYANOACRYLATES Sometimes known as super-glues, these adhesives make possible almost instant repairs to both hard materials, such as metal and glass and flexible materials such as synthetic rubbers.

A drop of cyanoacrylate looks like a drop of water but beware: it sticks at once and more or less for ever, so put your broken vase together right first time and be careful not to get it on your fingers! To clean off, use the special manufacturer's solvent.

EPOXY ADHESIVES Strong and versatile, epoxy resin comes in two parts, resin and hardener. Once equal parts have been mixed together setting is by chemical action which nothing can stop! It is ideal for repairs to metal, china and glass as, once set, it is unaffected by damp or heat.

The setting time varies from a few minutes to hours but is usually faster in warm conditions. The fast-acting epoxies are valuable for jobs where it would be difficult to hold the pieces in place for any length of time.

Remove spills quickly, before they set, with soapy water.

PVA (POLYVINYL ACETATE) Another really versatile adhesive, PVA glue is useful to have in the house; it keeps well and can be used safely by children as well as for a range of DIY jobs, from woodworking joints and sticking down hardboard to polystyrene ceiling tiles. This adhesive will not stick plastics and is only damp-resistant, not water resistant.

You can clean up any spills with water. Setting time is about half an hour.

STAIN
REMOVAL

CHIEF GUIDELINES

HOUSEHOLD SURFACES

LEATHER,
SUEDE AND SHEEPSKIN

GOOD
CLOTHES CARE

CHIEF GUIDELINES

A greasy mark on the front of your sweatshirt or grass stain on new cricketing trousers can make the heart sink. Instead of despairing, deal with the problem at once, if possible. The newer the stain the easier it is to remove, especially if you also tackle it in the correct way.

STAIN REMOVING KIT

For prompt treatment you really need to have ready to hand not only the soaps, salts and proprietary solvents that you will find recommended and described in the following pages but also a collection of clean pads, sponges and cloths to work with.

- Cut a large sponge into small pieces so that there is always a clean one to hand; use these to apply your remedial treatment.
- Fold old (clean) sheeting to make a pad to work over – so that you do not use the nearest tea towel and ruin that too.
- Keep cotton buds for precise application on tiny stains.
- A nail brush and an old toothbrush will help where small areas require attention.
- An old medicine dropper, well washed-out, is useful for dripping very small amounts of cleaner on to a small area or for squirting it through stained fabric so that the stain is removed on to a backing pad.

- Finally, a handful of paper tissues will quickly soak up a liquid that may cause a stain if it is left on and allowed to soak in.
- Keep your stain removing kit in something like a plastic box with a snap-on lid under the kitchen sink.

HOW TO 'SPONGE' A STAIN First, deal with the stain from the *wrong* side of the garment and use a clean cloth pad on the other side to absorb the substance of the stain as you remove it from the fabric. You are, in effect, pushing it from the surface of the fabric straight on to the pad and if any traces do remain behind they will be on the wrong side and thus not visible. Change the pad as soon as it becomes dirty.

Dampen a cloth or sponge with the cleaner and gently wipe this into the stain. Start by making a ring just around the stain, where the fabric is clean, then work inwards. If you begin in the middle you may leave an unsightly ring round the outside of the stain which may mean that the whole garment has to be washed or dry-cleaned. (If you do end up with a ring on a fast-coloured fabric, it can sometimes be removed by holding the area over the steam coming from a kettle.)

DOING MORE HARM THAN GOOD Some fabrics, such as acetates and viscose and some delicate and coloured materials may react unfavourably to cleaning chemicals so be sure to test cleaning agents out first on a hidden part, for instance on the inner hem or seam. If you have had several attempts at removing a stain but are not able to get rid of the last tiny traces, simply leave it; too much rubbing or chemical action is more likely to harm the fabric permanently than leave you with a perfectly spotless item.

SOAKING Once the household stand-by for dealing with stains and now back in fashion with the introduction of the biological soap powders, soaking can be a very useful method for removing stains. It works especially well with protein-based stains but is not suitable for wool, or garments with wool fibre in them, silk or fabrics with a flameproof finish. You may get the stain out but you will surely ruin the garment. (Never pour boiling water on wool items either.)

STAIN REMOVAL CHART

ADHESIVES

STICKY TAPE	Use methylated spirit.
CONTACT AND CLEAR ADHESIVE	Dab gently with acetone (or nail varnish remover) except on acetate fabrics.
EPOXY RESIN	Get to work before it sets. For natural fabrics, apply methylated spirit; for synthetics, use lighter fuel.
LATEX	Remove as much as possible before it dries – use cold water. Then peel off and dab any mark left with grease solvent.
MODELLING CEMENT	Remove with acetone or a non-oily nail varnish remover (except on acetate fabric).
PVA GLUE	Apply methylated spirit.
SUPERGLUE	Hold under running cold water or use a wet pad.

ALCOHOL

BEER	*Washables:* Rinse in lukewarm water, soak in biological washing powder, then wash. *Non-washables:* Blot up as much as possible, dab with white vinegar, blot again.
SPIRITS	*Washables:* Rinse in cold water. *Non-washables:* Blot up, sponge with methylated spirit. Blot, sponge with cold water.
RED WINE	*Washables:* Sponge immediately with white wine then treat as if white wine (see below). *Or* cover with salt to absorb wine then stretch material over a basin and pour through boiling water. *Non-washables:* Sponge with warm water and blot. Sprinkle with talcum powder and leave for an hour. Sponge and blot again.

WHITE WINE	*Washables:* Rinse in warm water, sponge with borax solution if necessary. If stain has dried, loosen with glycerine before laundering. *Non-washables:* As red wine.
BIRD DROPPINGS	*Washables:* Scrape off and soak in biological powder before washing as usual. For droppings coloured by berries, see Fruit juices. *Non-washables:* Scrape off, sponge with solution of 1 part ammonia to 6 parts water (test coloureds first). Soak up excess moisture; dab with white vinegar.
BLOOD	*Washables:* Soak in a strong salt and water solution for five minutes; rinse, soak again in clean solution. Repeat until the stain has gone. Soak stubborn stains in a solution of hydrogen peroxide plus ammonia (1 tablespoon 20 vol. strength hydrogen peroxide to 7 to 8 tablespoons water plus ½ tablespoon ammonia). Do not use on pure nylon. *Non-washables:* Soak up blood, then sponge with a few drops of ammonia in cold water. If traces still remain, apply a paste of starch and water. Let dry.
DRIED BLOOD	*Washables* (not wool or silk): Soak overnight in biological powder. *Non-washables:* Dampen with lemon juice, sprinkle with salt, iron between two sheets of slightly damp white blotting paper.

CANDLE WAX	Freeze affected item until wax is hard enough to scrape off. Cover stained area with clean white blotting paper and use a warm iron to remove the rest. Repeat ironing if necessary. Use a solvent for any last traces or methylated spirit for coloured wax.
CARBON PAPER	*Washables:* Sponge with undiluted liquid detergent and rinse well. If it persists, dab with methylated spirit then treat with liquid detergent and a few drops of household ammonia. *Non-washables:* Sponge repeatedly with white spirit or methylated spirit.
CHEWING GUM	*Washables:* Soften with egg white or grease solvent and scrape off, then wash. *Or* freeze till hard and peel off. Remove any residue by ironing over with brown paper or treat with methylated, or white spirit or proprietary chewing gum stain remover. *Non-washables:* Freeze and peel off, remove last traces with grease solvent.
CHOCOLATE	*Washables:* Scrape off any solids, then wash in cool soapy water. If necessary, sponge with a warm borax solution: 25g (1 oz) borax to 600 ml (1 pint) water. *Or* sponge with warm water, sprinkle with dry borax, rubbing it in gently and leave for half an hour. Rinse and launder as usual. Use a proprietary grease solvent if any stain lingers.

Non-washables: Scrape off, then use grease solvent.

COFFEE AND TEA

Washables: Rinse out in suds as soon as possible. If necessary, soak overnight in biological powder. For immediate results, sponge with warm borax solution (see Chocolate above). *Non-washables:* Sponge with borax solution, then blot. If necessary use a grease solvent.

CORRECTION FLUID (TIPPEX)

Washables: Allow to dry and pick off as much as possible. Dab stain with acetone or nail varnish remover, except on man-made fibres. For these, wash or take to dry cleaner. *Non-washables:* Allow to dry, pick off as much as possible, then dry clean.

CRAYON

Washables: Treat with methylated spirit then wash. *Or* rub with undiluted detergent and rinse thoroughly. Remove any remaining colour with methylated spirit. *Non-washables:* Dab with grease solvent or take to dry cleaner.

DYES

Washables: Add a few drops of ammonia to methylated spirit and sponge gently, but be sure to test first on coloureds or man-made fibres. *Or* rinse well in cold water and soak in biological detergent. Treat any remaining dye on white fabric with a proprietary dye stripper. *Non-washables:* Take to the dry cleaner immediately.

EGG	*Washables:* Scrape off solids, rinse in cold water, wash in biological powder. *Non-washables:* Scrape off solids, then treat with a grease solvent.
FOOD COLOURING	*Washables:* Sponge immediately with cold water, work in undiluted liquid detergent, then rinse. If stain remains, dab with methylated spirit. *Non-washables:* Sponge with cold water, then treat with methylated spirit.
FRUIT JUICES	*Washables:* Rinse in cold water. If colour remains, stretch garment over the basin and pour hot water through it. For beetroot, sprinkle powdered borax over stain before treating with hot water. *Non-washables:* Sponge with cold water, then with glycerine. Leave for an hour, then sponge with white vinegar. Finally, sponge with cold water.
GRASS AND LEAF STAINS	*Washables:* Wash in warm soapy water. If stain remains, sponge with methylated spirit and wash. *Non-washables:* Make up equal quantities of cream of tartar and salt into a paste with water and rub this into the stain. Leave for 15 minutes, then brush off.
GRAVY	*Washables:* Wash at once in cold soapy water. Rinse. Use a solvent to remove any greasy traces. *Non-washables:* Sponge with soapy water. Blot dry, then use a solvent.

GREASE

Most fabrics can be treated with a proprietary grease solvent. Sponge on the *wrong* side.

INK

BALLPOINT

Washables: Rub with warm soapy water, then wash. Use nail varnish remover for any stain that remains (except on acetates). *Non-washables:* Dab with nail varnish remover (except on acetates). Alternatively, use a proprietary ballpoint stain remover.

FELT-TIP

Washables: Remove as much as possible with pads of cotton wool or paper towels. Small spots can be dabbed with methylated spirit (except on acetates). Wash with soap powder or flakes and rinse well. Alternatively, use a proprietary felt-tip stain remover. *Non-washables:* Small spots can be tackled with methylated spirit, otherwise take to the dry cleaner.

FOUNTAIN PEN

Washables: Treat with liquid detergent as soon as possible. Rinse. Stretch fabric over a bowl, cover stain with salt and pour the juice of a lemon over it. Leave for at least 2 hours, then wash as usual. *Non-washables:* Sponge with cold water and blot well. Alternatively, use proprietary stain remover spray, or take to the dry cleaner.

INDELIBLE

Treat at once with a proprietary indelible ink stain remover.

TYPEWRITER	Sponge with methylated spirit and/or a dry cleaning solvent.
MAKE-UP LIPSTICK	*Washables:* Most stains will wash out. If stubborn, apply a suitable proprietary make-up stain remover. *Non-washables:* Apply a proprietary make-up stain remover.
MASCARA	*Washables:* Sponge with washing-up liquid, then with ammonia, and rinse out. *Non-washables:* Treat with a dry cleaning fluid.
METAL POLISH	Treat with white spirit. When stain is dry, brush gently to bring off any dried bits of polish.
MILDEW	*Washables:* If the usual wash does not remove it, soak in 1 part 20 vol. hydrogen peroxide to 6 parts water, but watch for possible bleeding of colour. *Non-washables:* Take to dry cleaners.
NAIL VARNISH	Simply dab with your varnish remover (except on acetates). If you are not sure what the fabric is, test on inside seam first or use amyl acetate.
PAINT OIL-BASED/ GLOSS/ENAMEL	*Washables:* Dab with white spirit or turpentine. Sponge with soapy water, then wash. *Non-washables:* As above but do not wash.
EMULSION/ WATER-COLOUR	Sponge with cold water. Dry cleaning may be necessary for delicate fabrics.

PERSPIRATION	*Washables:* If washing in a biological washing powder does not work, sponge with weak solution of ammonia, then rinse and wash. *Non-washables:* Sponge with a solution of 1 teaspoon white vinegar to 250 ml (8 fl oz) warm water.
PUTTY/PLASTICINE	*Washables:* Freeze until hard, scrape off as much as possible, then sponge with grease solvent. Wash. *Non-washables:* Freeze and scrape. Sponge with grease solvent. If stain remains, take to dry cleaner.
RUST	Sponge with a solution of 1 teaspoon oxalic acid to ½ litre (1 pint) water. (N.B. Oxalic acid is poisonous so be careful.)
SCORCH MARKS	*Washables:* Slight marking may be removed by soaking in cold milk. After this, if still necessary, dab with soapy water containing 1 teaspoon borax, then rinse out. *Non-washables:* Keep sponging with solution of 2 teaspoons borax in ½ litre (1 pint) warm water. Then sponge with cold water.
SHOE POLISH	Treat with white spirit or a dry cleaning fluid.
SUNTAN OIL	See Grease. If any colour remains after treating, soak washables in warm water with 1 teaspoon borax added, then wash in detergent and rinse well.

TAR AND OIL	*Washables:* Scrape off, then sponge from wrong side of fabric with eucalyptus oil. Remove any remaining traces with lighter fuel, then wash as usual. *Non-washables:* Scrape carefully. Loosen with glycerine, then rub gently with lighter fuel and dab with a cloth wrung out in warm water.
URINE	*Washables:* Soaking in biological powder is usually enough. *Non-washables:* Sponge with cold water and blot up, then sponge with a solution of 2 teaspoons white vinegar to 1 litre/1¾ pints water. (This will also help to banish any smell.)
VOMIT	*Washables:* Scrape, soak and wash in biological powder. *Non-washables:* Scrape and sponge repeatedly with warm water to which a few drops of ammonia have been added.

UPHOLSTERY AND CARPETS

The best way to deal with stains on carpets and upholstery is, of course, to prevent them happening in the first place. Some carpets have a special stain-resistant finish; spills are not absorbed by the carpet and can be mopped up easily.

Once something has been spilled on your carpet or cushions, even where there is a resistant finish, the first course of action must always be to blot it up as quickly as possible, not rubbing but pressing down with a wad of tissue or kitchen towel (stand on this if on the carpet) and replace with a fresh wad as soon as the first is soaked or stained. If you act fast enough this can prevent any lasting stain at all in some cases. In the same way, go to work on streaks and smears as soon as you notice them.

For individual stains, follow the stain removal chart given earlier in this chapter, adapting the instructions as necessary. Where you cannot 'rinse' your carpet, flush instead with soda water from a syphon or mop with a clean damp cloth. Where it says 'wash', use a special carpet shampoo. In general, avoid overwetting the carpet; blot up your cleaning liquid as you work.

For upholstery you will probably find the 'Non-washables' notes most useful. Some can also be treated with proprietary upholstery shampoo. Most fabrics can be shampooed, although some, such as cotton velvet, chenilles, tapestry, silk and wool are best left to the professional. Acrylic velvet and many other sofa coverings can be cleaned using the foam only from upholstery shampoo. This is available as a liquid that needs mixing with water or in an aerosol can with a brush attachment. Apply the foam (with a brush), wipe it over the fabric, allow to dry thoroughly and then vacuum off.

SHAMPOOING CARPETS Test first to make sure that the dye will not run. Apply some of the foam in an odd corner or on an offcut, brush in and cover with a white cloth; if the cloth picks up the colour, do not shampoo. If it does not, go ahead and spread the foam thinly and evenly over the whole carpet. Allow to dry, then vacuum off.

HOT WATER EXTRACTION CLEANING

Sometimes incorrectly described as steam cleaning, this is another alternative for cleaning carpets and upholstery. You can either employ professionals or do it yourself, hiring a special machine that you use rather like a vacuum cleaner, putting in water and a cleaning agent. The mixture is sprayed out and then sucked back, together with all the dirt from the furnishings you are treating. As with shampooing, beware of overwetting – and choose a fine day for your task, so that you can have the windows open to let everything dry out.

CHINA AND EARTHENWARE

Clean badly stained china by soaking it in neat domestic bleach for one to two days. Be sure to rinse well before use. (This method is quite harsh and may not be advisable for your fine china, rather for cooking bowls.) Stains on china will also sometimes respond to wood ash, used as a scourer. This is a gentler method; just rub the ash in with your fingertips, then wash thoroughly.

Earthenware, being porous, requires different treatment. Soak the article in distilled water until it cannot absorb any more. Then make up a paste of French chalk and distilled water and spread this on the stained area. Leave for a day: when the paste begins to crack off, just dust it away. If necessary, repeat. If the stain still remains, try rubbing with methylated spirit.

ELECTRICAL APPLIANCES

Usually it is sufficient simply to wipe with a cloth and non-abrasive cream but if careless use has resulted in plastic melting and sticking to the metal, use lighter fuel or nail varnish remover to get it off. Apply sparingly on a cloth and unplug the appliance first.

GLASSWARE

As wine and sherry decanters are used largely for show, it is important that they look sparkling clean. To remove any tidemarks or dregs stains, half-fill the decanter with water and add a handful of uncooked rice. Stop the top and hold firmly; swish the water and rice round until it has done its job. Rinse out with hot water.

Equally, the effect of a glass vase is spoiled if the inside has been stained by hard water during use. To clean, rub with a gentle scouring paste or pumice powder; pad a wooden spoon with a cloth and use this if you cannot get right into the vase. Wash in warm soapy water and rinse well.

PEWTER

Pewter does not rust as some other metals do, so it can be washed in warm soapy water. If a dull, dark film builds up, clean this off with ordinary metal polish. Use methylated spirit on a cloth for bad spots and stains or try fine wire wool dipped in olive oil, working *with* the lines of the article, e.g. round and round a bowl, rather than scrubbing in all directions.

SAUCEPANS

Pots and pans today are so attractive and versatile that they not only do service as cooking vessels but are often used at the table or displayed around the kitchen when not in use. It is certainly worth to keep them looking their best.

ENAMEL Fill the pan with cold water and add a tablespoonful of bleach, or 2 tablespoons for a large pan. Leave until the stain disappears, then rinse well before using again. For the outside, use an ordinary abrasive powder; remove slight staining by rubbing with a damp cloth dipped in bicarbonate of soda.

GLASS Burnt-on stains can be a problem with glass pans (which demand more effort than most pots and pans if they are to look really spotless). Soak for about an hour in a solution of 2 tablespoons of bicarbonate of soda in 1 litre (1¾ pints) of cold water.

STAINLESS STEEL It is not really stainless! Avoid 'rainbow' marks by not allowing the outside of the pan to overheat: use a radiant or gas ring of a slightly smaller diameter than that of the pan. Wash in hot soapy water and never use harsh metal scourers or scouring powders that might scratch the surface. Once soaking has removed any stubborn deposits, restore the appearance of your pan using a proprietary stainless steel cleaner or by wiping over with lemon juice or vinegar on a cloth.

HOUSEHOLD SURFACES

CANE

Popular for chairs, tables and even bedheads, cane is definitely 'easy-care'. Most dirty marks can be wiped off – use washing soda in warm water for unvarnished cane. To remove stains, apply a weak solution of household bleach.

CERAMIC HOB

Use one of the special hob cleaners to keep the finish in good condition, working only when the hob is cold. If stains persist, make a paste of the cleaner with water, apply this and leave to dry. Rinse off and dry before re-using the hob.

FLOORING

CORK Most things wipe off polyurethane or vinyl-sealed cork. For marks on a waxed cork floor, use a solvent-based floor polish.

LINOLEUM If washing the lino has not removed the stain that is bothering you, apply neat turpentine to it on a pad of cloth. Be careful not to use too much turpentine and do not pour it directly on to the lino.

QUARRY TILES You can be fairly tough on quarry tiles. For marks that do not disappear with the usual mopping or scrubbing with floor cleaner, use a paste of floor cleaner and water. Leave this on for 5 to 10 minutes, then scrub off. Restore old tiles that are looking a bit patchy, using fine wire wool and white spirit. Make sure the gas burners are off and that there are no naked flames in the room while you do the job and keep the room well aired. Work in small areas and mop up as you go.

VINYL Most marking is easily removed with a mop. For scratches, apply a little metal polish with a cloth. For the black streaks sometimes made by the heels of shoes, rub gently with a non-abrasive cream cleanser on a damp cloth – or use toothpaste!

IVORY

Most often met with in the piano! Whiten keys that have turned yellow by wiping with a cloth moistened with lemon juice. Ivory goes yellow more quickly in the dark, so leave the keyboard cover up when you have finished.

LAMINATES

Most kitchen worktops are now made of plastic laminate which does not stain easily. When there is a stain (turmeric makes an obstinate mark) use a cream kitchen cleanser or a little dry bicarbonate of soda on a damp cloth. Tea stains on white laminate can be treated with a mild bleach solution: 1 teaspoonful bleach to ½ litre (1 pint) water. Make sure that you rinse well afterwards and do not use on coloured or patterned surfaces or you may remove more than you intended.

LEATHER

Caution is necessary when treating the special finishes of leather furniture: clean according to the manufacturer's instructions. The main problem with leather desk-tops is usually ink and speed is essential in dealing with the spill or streak. Blot up quickly and wash the area with water for fountain pen ink or milk for ballpoint.

MARBLE

Marble, being porous, does stain readily. Use lemon juice to bleach out stains but be careful as the acid can damage the marble and you should rinse it off after only a couple of minutes. Repeat as necessary so long as the marble shows no sign of damage. For fume stains from the fire or from cigarettes, rub the marble with a cloth soaked in vinegar, then rinse well.

WALLPAPER

Wallpaper now comes with its own set of international care symbols and you should refer to these if it becomes marked. In general, use a spray dry cleaner for greasy marks; some other marks may come off if you rub gently with a soft artist's rubber or a piece of white bread.

You should be able to wipe even children's crayoning from vinyls but most wallpapers are trickier to deal with – even washable papers are really only spongeable (use a little washing-up liquid). Dab with bicarbonate of soda on a moist cloth to remove crayon marks or use dry cleaning fluid. Dry cleaning fluid can also be used for greasy stains. Alternatively, cover with clean white blotting paper and press gently with a warm iron. If adhesive tape has left a sticky shine, rub with a clean cloth soaked in lighter fuel.

Wherever possible try out your chosen method on a spare piece of paper first.

Leather, Suede and Sheepskin

When it comes to both day to day upkeep and occasional stain removal, leather, suede and sheepskin present a quite different set of problems from those of most other fabrics. For all their strength and versatility they are very vulnerable to most cleaning products.

LEATHER

BOOTS AND SHOES Remove any dirt from leather boots and shoes with a damp cloth, then polish well with a good wax polish.

A common stain on leather results from the salt spread on the roads to melt snow. You can get rid of these tidemarks by rubbing in a solution of half vinegar, half water. Leave to dry, then polish as usual.

Brown shoes stained by rain and patchy-looking will benefit from a rub with turpentine. Work it in and leave overnight, then polish.

GLOVES Remove dirty marks from kid gloves by rubbing gently with a soft clean eraser. It is probably easiest to do this with the glove on your hand. It is also possible to use bread: crumble white bread between your palms while wearing the glove and roll it round on the marked areas; it should pick up the dirt.

HANDBAGS AND BRIEFCASES Use colourless beeswax furniture polish to keep leather bags and cases looking good and to help prevent staining. You can also clean them with saddle soap. Apply this with a small sponge, working it in with a circular movement, then rinse it off with a cloth dipped in warm water. Leave to dry, then polish.

COATS AND JACKETS Wipe off any surface dirt with a soft cloth but do not attempt to treat stains at home. Solvents will almost always remove the colour from the leather as well as the original mark. Take the coat to a dry cleaner who specializes in leather and if possible let them know what caused the stain, as this may help them deal with it satisfactorily.

It is expensive but well worthwhile to have leather garments cleaned regularly, before they become too soiled.

SUEDE

Although suede also requires professional cleaning, it is sometimes possible to deal with the odd mark at home. Rub Fuller's earth into the mark and leave for 15 minutes before brushing out with a soft brush (not a wire brush). Do not use any sort of chemical fluid as it may ruin the colour of the suede or, at least, leave an unsightly ring.

SHEEPSKIN

Sheepskin should also be professionally cleaned but, as with suede, the occasional mark can be removed by using Fuller's earth. Rub it in well and brush off after about an hour. You can also freshen up the woolly side with dry hair shampoo (follow the manufacturer's instructions, i.e. spray or sprinkle it on, then leave for a while and brush or shake out).

SHEEPSKIN RUG Use the lather only from a bowl of soapflakes in warm water. Work it in with a brush but do not be over energetic and be careful not to overwet the rug. Dry away from direct heat, then vacuum.

GOOD CLOTHES CARE

SUCCESSFUL WASHING

Good washing practice requires just a little forethought and planning in the way you sort, prepare and complete your wash.

PRECAUTIONS Check over all garments for objects left in pockets, up sleeves before you put them in. Turn clothes inside out to minimize fading and close zips so that the fabric overlap protects them.

To check an item for colour fastness, try it out

first in warm soapy water in the sink; if the colour runs, wash separately. Or dip a part of the article in the water then place between two sheets of blotting paper on the ironing board and press with a warm iron. If the colour either comes through on to the paper or alters to any extent as the iron heats it, wash separately.

SORTING Do this properly – and not just in the old-fashioned way of 'whites' and 'coloureds'. You can wash articles with different care labels on one programme, so long as this is chosen to suit the most delicate item to be included. The same rule applies if the label lists only fibre content with no specific washing instruction (often on imported goods): wash according to the most vulnerable fibre listed.

PRE-TREATING If a shirt has dirty collar and cuffs or cotton trousers are grimy round the pockets, give them a head start by soaping and scrubbing these before they go into the wash. Use either ordinary bar soap or a universal stain-removing bar.

Although washing machines usually carry a pre-wash option, soaking the item in advance is helpful where you do not want to pre-wash the whole load.

Soak whites overnight and coloured articles for 2 to 3 hours. Use hand-hot, not boiling, water and never soak wool or silk or anything that may not be colourfast. Some fabrics with special finishes, e.g. showerproof or flame-resistant, are damaged by soaking, as are garments with metal trimmings.

LOADING Follow the manufacturer's instructions as to the load your machine will take and still do its job – if the load cannot rotate freely it will not be either washed or rinsed properly. Allow more space if the wash is an especially dirty one.

DETERGENT Always buy the *type* suggested. If you have an automatic you will get better performance with a low-lather powder; with ordinary powder the froth can fill up the drum and prevent good washing and rinsing just as if you had put in too large a load. By using ordinary powder you may also seriously damage the machine.

Avoid using biological detergents for baby

clothes or if anyone in the family suffers from eczema or has a very sensitive skin; it is thought that they can irritate this.

WHITENERS Proprietary whiteners can be added to the wash if you have particular items that demand brightening up. Follow the instructions on the container.

FABRIC CONDITIONERS These not only serve to keep washing soft to the touch but can also reduce the build-up of static electricity in synthetics such as nylon and polyester and help to get rid of perspiration odours in the wash.

VINEGAR If washing is not properly rinsed for any reason, for instance when too much soap has been used, re-rinse after adding a cupful of ordinary white vinegar to the water.

LABELLING AND WASHING SYMBOLS

Always use the recommended care label advice. Washing symbols on care labels in this country are accompanied by explanatory words. The five basic outline symbols are:

WASHING

The three variables in the washing process (water temperature, agitation and spinning) are indicated by the tub symbols. Maximum water temperature is shown in degrees celsius inside the tub. Agitation and spinning are both shown by the use of a bar or broken bar under the tub:

 Single bar denotes reduced machine action (agitation and water extraction)

 Broken bar denotes the much reduced machine action necessary for machine washable wool (with normal spinning)

 Hand wash only. Do not machine wash.

CHLORINE BLEACHING

A triangle containing the letters Cl indicates that the article may be treated with chlorine bleach. If it is crossed out this means that chlorine bleach must not be used. The symbol refers to chlorine bleach only and not to other types of bleach. It is most likely to appear on articles labelled on the continent where chlorine bleach is more commonly used than in the UK.

 TUMBLE DRYING, AFTER WASHING

Most textile articles can be safely tumble dried: Watch for articles which may be harmed by tumble drying (e.g. articles containing foam rubber and most wool knitwear).
(Where tumble drying is prohibited, extra instructions, e.g. 'dry flat' should be given in words.)
Where dots appear: • • means high setting, • means low setting.

IRONING

There are four variations. The temperatures shown in brackets are the maximum sole plate temperatures indicated by the dots in the symbol.

 Hot (200°C) Cotton, linen, viscose or modal (modified viscose)

 Warm (150°C) Polyester mixtures, wool

 Cool (110°C) Acrylic, nylon, acetate, triacetate, polyester

 DO NOT IRON Where ironing would be bad for the fabric. (Does *not* indicate that ironing is not necessary.)

In addition to the symbol the words 'Cool', 'Warm' or 'Hot' may also appear on the label.

 DRY CLEANING

The circle means that the garment can be dry cleaned. However it should never appear on its own but with additional information to indicate which types of cleaning solvent may be used.

HOUSEHOLD PESTS

ESCAPING INVASION

Very few houses or flats, however well built and properly maintained, can hope to escape completely from the invasion of 'household pests'.

Many of the creatures are casual wanderers from the great outdoors, attracted in by the presence of warmth and food, for instance ants, wasps and mice. Others may indicate a point of weakness in the house: if you have a persistent problem with woodlice, you would do well to investigate the cause of the dampness in the plaster or woodwork that your woodlice are happily feeding and breeding on. Yet others may indicate that you have a problem with hygiene, either within the home or outside it.

Not that finding fleas in the carpet means that you and your family are dirty. And mice will occasionally appear in immaculate kitchens!

It is important to keep a sense of proportion when dealing with household pests.

Prevention is easier than cure. Do not let *your* home be the one that attracts or allows entry to pests. The following pages deal with pests individually but a few general points apply.

● Never leave scraps of food around. Sweep up crumbs after each meal and do not let children eat crisps and apples all over the house, leaving tasty morsels under beds, and so on.

• Put away or cover all food when you are not actually eating. This includes the pet food; instead of leaving it there all day, wait till the cat or dog asks for more. Make sure you keep the lid firmly on the dustbin. Flies will lay eggs on any foodstuffs in or out of the dustbin – indeed on both in turn – and rats delight in an open bin when they come out at night.

A TO Z OF PESTS

ANTS These are a common nuisance in the kitchen, making straight for the larder. They like protein, fatty foods and anything sweet, and will pass the message back to all their friends. Ordinary black garden ants are the usual invaders and are not a problem to deal with. Watch to see where the nest is when they return outside, if you can, then pour boiling water over it. Repeat if necessary. There are several proprietary products that will kill ants, maybe not so quickly but more thoroughly. Some powders work straightaway – but do not use these near areas where food is prepared or eaten. Others consist of a poisoned jelly bait which the ants eat and also take back to the nest for the queen and young of the colony – all are thus destroyed.

If you cannot find or reach the nest and the ants keep coming in, look for their point of entry and stuff it with cotton wool soaked in paraffin. Or paint an insecticidal coating on to the door threshold, and on the skirting. You can use a solution made by mixing 2 cups of borax with 1 cup of sugar and water. Spread this, outside, around the house. It will both attract the ants and kill them at the same time.

NOTE

The solution of borax, sugar and water may be tempting to small children so do not use this method if they are around. Also, with jelly bait, put it where children cannot stick in their fingers – out of curiosity perhaps – or, if they are in the garden a lot, put it out after their bedtime.

BEDBUGS Objects of repulsion to anyone unlucky enough to see them, bedbugs are minute brown, round, flat, wingless insects that live anywhere in old houses – behind peeling wallpaper, in cracked plaster or woodwork – as well as in bed mattresses. They are not common today because of modern standards of hygiene but may enter your home when you buy an old piece of upholstered furniture or they may have been lurking in cracks in the floor for some time.

Active at night and shy of light, bedbugs leave a small, itchy bite. They used to be dealt with by fumigating but this is used mainly for infested furniture today, persistent insecticide being the preferred treatment. Spray wherever you think the bedbugs seem to be in residence. Treat not only the affected mattress but the whole bed frame as well (do not saturate the mattress).

If you are confused or feel that the problem is out of your control, contact your local health authority for advice and assistance.

BEETLES Some beetles, such as the bread beetle and spider beetle, are sometimes found in stored food. Others may have simply come in by chance from the garden. Remove any infested food and clean thoroughly where this was kept. Aerosol or powder insecticides are available to dispose of the creatures at all stages of their life cycle.

Carpet beetles Though not well known by name, carpet beetles are in fact found fairly often, typically in airing cupboards or anywhere warm and dry where they can find their preferred food of carpet, feathers or wool.

The adults are small and oval, rather like a brown and yellow ladybird but it is the larvae that are the true pest. Again golden brown, these 'woolly bear' grubs eat small round holes in the carpet or whatever furnishings they are living in.

To get rid of them, spray with a persistent insecticide (the larvae can often survive treatment with a short-life preparation) and dust between the floorboards and under the carpet underlay (if possible) with an insecticidal powder.

As a preventive, clean carpets regularly and spray the folded-over edges of fitted carpets and usually undisturbed areas under heavy furniture with a residual insecticide. Spray also into floor-boards and in the thick seams of soft furnishings.

Plaster beetles Very small, dark beetles, these feed on the moulds and mildew that grow on damp walls, as do their larvae. They tend to occur where there is damp plaster in both old and new houses. The solution is to destroy the moulds by thoroughly heating and airing the room or rooms. Use a plaster beetle sighting as a warning that you have a damp problem somewhere.

COCKROACHES Cockroaches favour warm, moist spots around pipes, sinks and stoves and usually make their appearance in older properties where there are plenty of inaccessible hiding places. They appear at night and eat a wide variety of human food as well as various fabrics and paper. They also spread food poisoning, infecting where they walk.

Cockroaches can be very difficult to wipe out, so be thorough in your treatment if you have ever seen them in your home. You really do need to get the insecticide right into the places where they hide and it is not always easy to do this. Follow the instructions on the container and refer to these for any safety precautions with regard to food, children and pets.

EARWIGS Earwigs are usually seen only at night and do no real harm in the home. They do not live naturally indoors but come in from the garden, often in cut flowers or by chance from creepers growing around the house walls.

Sweep them up and throw them outside. If a number have settled in wall or floor crevices and they bother you, use an insecticide powder.

FLEAS These are more common than many people would like to think, and they mostly arrive on cats or dogs. Once associated with poverty and dirt, fleas are enjoying a new boom as they breed happily in our centrally heated, wall-to-wall carpeted homes – perfect conditions for them.

Cat fleas will actually infest human beings but dog fleas tend to stay with dogs. Both cause areas of great irritation around a red spot where the flea has bitten – further apart than mosquito bites and often in a line. Check your pet regularly for fleas.

You should be able to see the fleas running about in the fur – under the chin is a good place to look as the fleas apparently pass that way to seek moisture from the animal's mouth. The base of the tail is another popular spot. Fleas are tiny brownish creatures with powerful back legs, much larger than the rest of their body, which they use to jump from one host to another. (If one jumps on you, try to trap it by patting it with a soft bar of soap if there is one to hand, but you will have to be quick.)

The eggs look rather like dandruff and show that the animal is well infested. Get a good powder or spray from a vet and treat according to the manufacturer's instructions. Do not de-infest young kittens (under four months) or nursing mothers as it may adversely affect them.

Treat your pet's bedding at the same time as you treat the animal and give the animal a flea collar to wear to discourage further infestation. You can also treat upholstery and carpets. Vacuum thoroughly to pick up any stray fleas or eggs as they can lie dormant for long periods.

If the problem gets out of hand, contact the local authority, who will advise and help you.

FLIES Often no more than idly swatted away, flies are a serious pest that should be taken far more seriously than they are. They are prolific carriers of bacteria, not only walking over your food and food preparation area just as they earlier walked over germ-covered rubbish and rotting meat but also both vomiting and excreting on them as they feed. Flies can carry 30 different diseases and lay their eggs at an alarming rate during the summer months.

The problem is far more noticeable in some areas than in others but whether flies are an occasional or a constant bother, take action so that they can do no harm. As well as following the general principles mentioned above, discourage flies from frequenting your dustbin by washing it out regularly and disinfecting it. When dry, sprinkle with soap powder or drop in a mothball. Most important, make sure that the lid fits closely and *keep it on.* Keep any garden compost or manure well away from the house as flies will swarm to this. In fact, deprive the beasts of their breeding sites and deny them access to food.

If you still have trouble, get rid of flies by using a spray or a fly swat or hang up old-fashioned fly-papers (well out of the reach of children, and high enough not to catch on your hair) or plastic strips impregnated with insecticide. Alternatively, keep them away by using herbs.

● Rub woodwork round windows with oil of lavender which they dislike and will avoid.

● Place herb 'parcels' of cloves, camomile, basil and mint around the house.

● Hang a branch of bay leaves in the larder or food cupboard; you can use the leaves for cook-ing too.

MICE Sweet as they might be as pets (some would say), mice are definitely a real pest when living wild in the home. They qualify on two major fronts: contamination and gnawing.

They contaminate far more food than they actually eat and carry many diseases, particularly salmonella (food poisoning). Because of their preference for nibbling a little here and there rather than tucking into any one item, the chances of their infecting any foodstuffs available to them are high.

As for gnawing, mice are rodents and have to keep on and on chewing at things to maintain their sharp little incisors at the same length. Any-thing will do and this may well include such household hardware as electric cables, wood of any sort and even gas pipes, as well as cardboard boxes, newspapers, and so on. Signs that you have mice around include chewed packets, scratching and scuffling behind the skirting board and trails of little hard brown dropping in-side cupboards, on the fridge, and round the rub-bish bin. Most offenders will be grey house mice with the occasional long-tailed field mouse look-ing for food and a nesting site.

If you suspect that mice have arrived in the home do not delay taking action. They breed rapidly and can constitute a serious problem. A cat in residence usually puts off mice – just the smell does the trick. If you have no cat, try 'bor-rowing' one for a few weeks – it might even catch something! If you have got a cat and it is not doing its job, put out traps at night; either spring them in the morning and reset at night or make sure that you put them where *no one* (not even the cat) can accidentally set them off and catch fingers or noses. The best bait is said to be chocolate; or try nuts and peanut butter. Cheese is not the best choice, contrary to all the stories.

If traps do not have the desired effect, put down poison, again where it cannot be reached by inquisitive children, although the dosage, mixed as it is with oatmeal, is too low to hurt humans or pets. Check with the container instructions (but, in any case, always keep remaining poison locked away).

You can, of course, simply try to stop the mice getting in. If they are using pipe runs as entries for instance, screw up wire wool or chicken wire and stuff it in the gaps; it may do the trick. Or, deter the mice another way: soak balls of paper in oil of peppermint and put these in their entrance/exits. Or place sprigs of fresh mint where they have been visiting; they are said not to like the smell and will keep away from it.

MITES A variety of mites live in the house. They are not true insects and are so small that they are seldom seen unless one happens to catch the eye when it moves. Because of this, their numbers can grow unnoticed until they suddenly seem to have appeared everywhere.

Food mites Throw away any affected food; air and dry out the cupboard.

House or furniture mites They favour old upholstery, especially if it is a bit damp. Turn up the heating and expose the mites to hot, dry air for 24 hours; this should get rid of them.

Dust mites These are everywhere and are harmless although unfortunately some people are allergic to them. If someone in your household is allergic, vacuum regularly; it may help.

Gooseberry red spider mites Though they are actually garden pests, they sometimes come into the house. Discourage them by using an insecticide around the doors and windows where you think they may be entering and cut back any nearby greenery.

MOSQUITOES Not as serious here as in many other countries, mosquitoes are still a pest, especially when a lone female (females are the biters) gets into your bedroom at night. If you have a stagnant puddle, pond or even water butt where they breed, a drop of paraffin on the surface of the water will prevent the larvae from developing.

Light candles if you are having a barbecue and mosquitoes are bothering you out of doors. Indoors, keep a pot of fresh basil in the room – they dislike it.

MOTHS The moths themselves are not a pest but their larvae definitely are. They feed on natural fibres, especially wool and are even capable of eating just the wool from a wool-synthetics mix!

The larvae are most usually found in stored clothes and blankets – if the clothes are hanging, within the folds of the garment – and are covered by a fluffy substance. Brush them off the fabric, checking underneath collars and pocket flaps. If you find signs of moth larvae in a carpet, kill them by steam ironing with a warm iron and a damp cloth. Do not press down hard with the iron but let the steam do the job. There are aerosol products that you spray on to carpets to prevent any further damage.

Once you have discovered the larvae in one item in a drawer or wardrobe, check every item carefully. Prevent moths returning by lining drawers with newspaper (so that the larvae cannot creep back in through the bottom) and using mothballs. Things that are to be put away for a long time can be sprinkled with Epsom salts and, finally, if you are storing knitting wool for some time, wind it round a ball of camphor; it may smell a bit but it will not be eaten away.

The smells that attract moths are those of greasy stains, so never put away anything that is not perfectly clean.

RATS Man's ancient enemy! Rats have plagued man for most of history and still represent a grave health risk, as they carry many diseases. They will make their nests wherever rubbish is left lying around and appear wherever food is readily available. Rats are larger than mice and are not a pretty sight: they have longer tails and grow up to 23 cm (9 inches) long. There are two types of common rat, the sewer rat and the water rat. Like mice, rats also need to wear down their incisor teeth continually by gnawing and will set to work on wood, pipework and electric wiring.

Buy a good rat poison from the chemist or hardware shop and follow the instructions on the container. Use with care, especially if there are children or pets around. The only trouble with these poisons is that the creature may die just under the hearth or by a radiator where it will decompose and smell in the warmth while you are unable to get at it.

If you cannot solve the problem yourself, contact the local pest control officer; the local authority have an obligation to deal with rats as a health hazard. If you do succeed in killing a rat, or your cat does, burn it or bury it in the garden.

SILVERFISH Not a fish but a primitive wingless insect, small with a cigar-shaped body, the silverfish darts about very fast when disturbed. It is typically found in the bath or other damp places such as under the kitchen sink or in the back of unventilated cupboards. Silverfish eat carbohydrate – starch – where they can find it, in the glue of book bindings, or wallpaper paste, for instance. They can do quite a lot of damage to old books but, on the whole, do little harm. Keep them under control with a puff of insecticidal powder or sprinkle a mixture of boric acid and sugar in places they favour. (Do not use boric acid where children or pets may be tempted to touch it.)

SPIDERS Though they are the very essence of the hate, creepy-crawly, there is really no need to worry about spiders; in fact they do more good than harm.

If you do not want them in the house, remove them by trapping in a paper bag or lifting up on a brush or broom and simply dropping them out of doors. Alternatively, place a glass over the spider; allow it to crawl up the glass, cover the top with a sheet of paper and take it outside – if you put the glass down the spider will soon crawl out again.

Get rid of the webs using a damp cloth draped

over a broom or just vacuum them up.

TICKS Usually associated with the country and farm animals, ticks do make an occasional appearance on a family pet or even on a child in town or city surroundings. They are about 6 mm (¼ in)long and swell up with the blood they take as they bite. It is useful to know what to do if you find one.

Do not try to pull it off. You will probably break it, leaving the jaws embedded in the skin and this may lead to infection. Instead, soak cotton wool in methylated spirit and take hold of the tick with this. The spirit will make the tick release its hold and you can ease it off in one go. If you cannot face doing this, see a doctor or a vet.

WASPS AND BEES

Wasps Whether nesting in or out of the house they can be a worry, especially in late summer when they are rather dozy.

If you can get to it, treat a wasps' nest with a special wasp killer, puffing it into the entrance at dusk when the wasps are all safely inside. Wear gloves anyway as a precaution and move away as soon as you have finished in case there is any response. You can also make an old-fashioned wasp trap by hanging a jam-jar half-filled with jammy or sugary water somewhere near the nest.

Bees We are more sympathetic to bees. If a swarm settles in your house or garden, contact the local council or a beekeeping association for someone to come and take it away in a basket. It is a job for an expert; do not tackle a swarm yourself unless you know what you are doing.

WEEVILS There are different types of weevils, but the most common in the home are those found in flour or bread. Others eat wood (see Woodworm). If you discover these tiny beetles in a bag of flour or bran return it to the shop; if you have only just bought it, it might be a good idea to report this to the local health authority.

Clean out the cupboard and spray with insecticide, taking care not to pollute any food.

WOODLICE Harmless in themselves, these tiny grey crustaceans are a sure sign of damp. Get rid of them with an insecticide but, more important, look for and treat the source of the damp.

WOODWORM The first sign of the presence of woodworm is usually little piles of fresh sawdust and holes in the woodwork or furniture. Both are made by the grubs of the wood-boring furniture beetle which lays eggs on the surface of the wood. When the grubs hatch they bore into the wood leaving no sign of entry and may stay in there for up to ten years. When ready, the larva makes its way to just below the surface and then the hatched beetle bores its way out, leaving the tell-tale refuse and the flight holes.

Woodworm attack both new and old wood so beware when you buy any secondhand or antique furniture that there are no signs of recent activity – though this is not easy. You can treat small items yourself with a proprietary liquid which you usually squirt into the holes. Follow any manufacturer's instructions precisely. Do not inhale the fumes or let the fluid splash on your skin. Wash off immediately, if it does.

Larger areas will need thorough spraying and it may be a good idea to get professional advice.

OTHER UNWELCOME VISITORS

BATS The many bats that live and breed in this country are mainly insect-eating and do absolutely no harm at all to man or beast. They are mammals, warm-blooded creatures, and since 1981 have been protected by law in this country under the Countryside Act. Some species are in danger of dying out and the part of this legislation that may affect you concerns what you may or may not do if you have bats living on your premises. You may not get rid of them by any means nor block their access. It is also forbidden to treat the premises (usually the roof space of a house) with any chemical that might hurt the bats living there and this would probably include treatments for such things as woodworm and dry rot.

You do not have to provide a home for the bats for ever; if you do want to spray your attic or convert it into an extra room, contact the Nature

Conservancy Council and they will send a representative along. He or she will arrange for the bats to be moved, at an appropriate time – not for instance in the middle of their breeding season.

You can be prosecuted if it is discovered that you have ignored this law.

SQUIRRELS These are not protected by law and can prove quite a nuisance if they settle in your roof. Do not harm the squirrels. Be patient and wait until all the brood is out looking for food, then go up and block up their entrance holes with chicken wire and mortar.

CATS AND DOGS Dogs and cats may be much-loved pets but both often qualify as pests as well, in their own homes and gardens and even more in those of their neighbours.

Cats A cat digging where you have just planted out seedlings is enough to infuriate any gardener and whether it is your cat or your neighbour's does not make a lot of difference. Use cotton wound round sticks to crisscross vulnerable borders, or wire netting, while seeds get going and sprinkle the ground with one of the proprietary cat repellants.

Deter visits from any tom cat who prefers to spray his territorial marker under *your* window by spraying him with water. If he persists, wash the area with hot, soapy water but do not try to wipe out the smell with bleach, it is more likely to attract him back. Spray the wall with a soda siphon after washing instead.

If local cats take advantage of your catflap replace it with the sort that requires a magnetic 'key' to open it – a special tag on your cat's collar.

Dogs Cats are almost impossible to train or limit, even with the best of intentions on the part of their owners but dogs should and can be kept under control. The dog not only is a pest but serves to encourage other household pests when its owner allows it to use the garden as a toilet without cleaning up the mess. This results in a filthy breeding ground for flies, as well as being offensive with regard to both sight and smell. If you have this problem with a neighbour and tactful approaches on the subject have no effect, ask the environmental health officer for help.

KNOWING WHAT TO DO – AND DOING IT SAFELY

To get rid of most household pests, it is necessary to turn to chemicals, often made up as proprietary products in the form of baits, puffers and aerosol sprays. You may also use an insecticidal smoke or fumigant. Whatever you choose, it is essential that you follow a few safety rules when using these.

• Always read the manufacturer's instructions carefully and follow them precisely. Do not be casual about this.

• Store all chemicals, during and after use, where children cannot possibly reach them.

• Never decant pest control chemicals into old lemonade bottles that might mislead children into thinking they have found a forgotten bottle, ideal for a secret swig. It seems obvious but it does happen.

• Always label bottles, jars or tins. It may be a while before you need that substance again and it is all too easy to forget what is what. Using the wrong chemical can be dangerous.

• Always take care when handling chemicals. Wear rubber gloves if possible; if you do splash your skin, wash it at once and always wash your hands anyway once you have finished the job, especially if you are about to eat a meal or prepare food for the family.

• Most sprays are both highly toxic and inflammable. Avoid inhaling the vapour from aerosols and always use in a well-ventilated room, making sure that pets and children are well out of the way. Keep clear of food and afterwards clean any nearby work surfaces. Never smoke when spraying or have any naked flames alight.

• Before using an aerosol, make sure the spray hole is pointing in the right direction and away from you. When it is finished, dispose of it safely; never puncture the can or place on a fire because it will explode.

• Flush any left-over liquid chemicals down an outside drain if you do not want to keep them, then pour buckets of cold water after them.

SAFETY FIRST

IS YOUR HOME SECURE?

FIRE HAZARDS

PERSONAL SAFETY

IS YOUR HOME SECURE?

House theft is on the increase everywhere and there will always be thieves happy to steal the videos, stereo systems and colour televisions so many households own or rent today, as well as those eager to pick up the surprisingly large amounts of cash people often seem to keep in the house and the one good silver watch or gold chain they own.

It *can* happen to you, so set to and think in a positive way about making your home more secure. The best way to start is probably to work out how you would try to get into the house yourself, if you were locked out. Which window catch can be slipped with a knife? Can you reach the bathroom window with the ladder from the garden shed? How obvious is the 'hiding place' for your spare front-door key? Any way that you can get in may be used by someone else more experienced than you in the ways and means of entering a property *not* by the front door.

Make a list of the weak points of the house as you see them then, if you feel you would benefit from some expert advice, contact the crime prevention officer at the local police station.

You can also sometimes call on your insurance company for advice. It may be that if you live in a high-risk area or have a valuable collection of some sort, your insurance company will approach *you* with specific security requirements. For example, they may insist that you fit special door locks and window catches as part of the insurance deal. You may even get a reduction in your premium if your home security arrangements are above a certain standard.

Finally, a reputable locksmith (in some areas locksmiths actually register with the police) can be a valuable source of practical suggestions – but remember that it is in his interests to sell you expensive products, which your situation may not warrant. Do not employ anyone about whom you have the slightest doubt.

Whatever you decide, do approach the task sensibly. It is one thing to take reasonable precautions but don't go over the top; there is no need to turn the place into Fort Knox – who wants to live in a vault? A really determined burglar will get in almost anywhere; it is the passing opportunist, the most common offender, you are aiming to keep out (very often these opportunists are juveniles, so don't think that just because *you* can't shin up a drainpipe or fit through the coal hole, no thief can).

What is more, you must always bear in mind that you might at some time need to leave the house in a hurry. The famous example is of the fixed double glazing that may keep out burglars (as well as cold) but also stops you breaking out in case of fire. If you fit window locks, make sure that everyone, including overnight visitors and your children, knows where the keys are kept: a good idea is to fix the key to the window frame with masking tape somewhere that no one outside can see it.

LOCKS

DOORS Police records show that the majority of house break-ins are made possible by inadequately secured doors and windows. On all outside doors fit a strong mortise deadlock: a lock with a bolt that, once thrown, cannot be forced out, so that you must use the key. It fits into a slot cut in the door, the bolt passing into another slot in the door post and is the most

KEEPING OUT BURGLARS

Windows:
Close and firmly latch all windows, especially on the ground floor, before going out. Upstairs windows near trees, drainpipes, flat roofs or other possible access points, should have good-fitting locks.

The front doorstep:
Before going on holiday arrange for a neighbour to gather up post, circulars, newspapers etc. so they do not pile up, alerting people to the fact that there is no-one in the house. Do not forget to cancel the milk.

Ladders:
If your ladder will not fit in the shed, keep it securely padlocked to a solid object outside.

Keys:
Never leave door keys hanging in the lock or 'hidden' under doormats or flowerpots or inside handy drainpipes – they are not hidden from anyone really looking for them. Do not keep address labels on keys: lost, labelled keys could lead any would-be thief straight to your house.

Doors and gates:
Securely lock or padlock garage and shed doors and side gates. Tools left in an unlocked garden shed make levering open a door or window the work of seconds. Inside doors leading from the garage into the house should have additional security.

Hedges and fences:
Keep hedges well trimmed so they do not obscure the view of doors and windows from the street. Fences, too, should not be so high that anyone trying to break in could hide behind them.

secure type of lock. There are various versions, including one suited to glazed doors, a two-bolt type with a knob or handle on each side and a purely key-operated or cylinder mortise lock for use in conjunction with a rim latch lock. Fitting a mortise lock is not difficult but does involve careful measurement and precise cutting of lock slots and key hole.

If you live in a flat, where the entrance door is the only really vulnerable spot, you may feel it is worth fitting a multi-point mortise lock which throws bolts into all four sides at once.

Remember that locks and bolts are often only as good as the screws that hold them; use long screws, not the tiny ones often supplied in kits.

If you have only a rim latch lock, this can easily be opened by slipping in a thin piece of plastic such as a credit card. You can prevent this happening by knocking a few carpet tacks into the frame just in front of the bolt recess. Do not knock them in all the way, just far enough for the door to close without scraping them. In this position they will block any attempt to slip the lock. However, the best solution would be to fit a mortise deadlock for extra security.

DOORS, DOOR SURROUNDS AND WINDOWS

WOODEN DOORS The very best door lock will do little good if the door itself is weak and can be easily forced open with a crowbar or a well-aimed kick. An exterior timber door should be made of wood at least 45 mm (2 inches) thick and preferably of hardwood such as mahogany, oak or teak.

Check that the door is in good condition and the door hinges firm and secure.

Inspect the door surround also; make sure it is sound – not split or rotten or coming away from the wall. Replace or refix to the wall as necessary.

Where you have two locks to the door, maximize their effect by placing one a third of the way from the top and the other a third of the way from the bottom of the door. This will help to provide extra strength against simple kicking-in of the door.

METAL AND GLAZED DOORS Metal-framed doors
are usually very strong; their main weakness is in
their glazed area. In fact this is true of most doors
and generally the larger the amount of glass, the
greater the risk – except that more than one blow
to break glass (just to put a hand through to reach
a catch) can make a lot of noise and so is not
popular with housebreakers.

You can lessen the risk by using toughened,
laminated or wired glass in a door. Laminated
glass is particularly good as it has a thin core of
plastic that remains in place even when the glass
is shattered and is very hard to break through.

WINDOWS Here you may not wish to have wired
glass but toughened or laminated safety glass (as
mentioned above) is excellent for use in high-risk
positions. Even fitting ordinary glass in a thicker
group gauge can improve window security.

Also, as with doors, look to the general good
condition of window frames and surrounds and
repair or replace as necessary. Keep puttied windows in good repair; cracked old putty is easily
prised off so that the pane can be removed.

KEEP THE BURGLAR OUT

Ask for identification whenever a stranger calls,
even if he says he is from the council or the gas
board or doing a survey. Many burglars carry
out thefts by tricking their way in and genuine
callers will understand your concern and not be
offended if you challenge them.

DOOR VIEWER In addition, fit a door viewer and
use it to look at your visitor before you open the
door, or even before you let him know that you
are in (if you have an unglazed door).

DOOR CHAIN These are also valuable if you are
not sure who is at the door. You can keep them
on, for instance, while checking an identity card,
before you actually open or close the door. But
they are only as strong as their fixings, so use
good, long screws and put them into solid wood
on both door and frame.

Some chains are lockable and cannot be opened
except with a key – a useful addition in case
someone tries to put a hand round the door and
release the chain.

There are many other things you can do to keep out intruders, ranging from keeping a dog (the bark is probably more use than the bite), fitting and using old-fashioned internal shutters (good for insulation, too) and using automatic devices to mislead them.

TIMESWITCH When you go out for the evening, set up an automatic timeswitch in the sitting-room and/or bedroom before you go. A timeswitch plugs into the wall socket and you then plug into it your table lamp and set the timer to go on and off at various times over the next few hours. Timeswitches operate either on a 24-hour or 7-day programme and some of the latter will also work randomly, turning the light on and off at different times each day.

You can also plug in a radio to further the impression that someone is at home. These switches are not expensive.

BURGLAR ALARMS

Alarm systems can play a valuable role, especially in giving the household a feeling of security but they should not be used as a substitute for strong locks and good preventive habits.

Burglar alarms act as a deterrent – the burglar may just give your house a miss when he sees the metal box up on the wall – and as a warning to you if you are at home, to neighbours and to the police if not. But consider carefully whether an alarm is worth installing in your particular situation. Assuming that the burglar is *not* put off before he starts and does *not* run away as soon as the alarm goes off, who would notice and take action if you were not at home? If you live somewhere remote or somewhere that is deserted during the day, neighbours will not be able to help and in busy streets alarm bells are often ignored by passers-by and cursed by neighbours, fed up with the constant false alarms given by so many systems. Of course, you can have the alarm connected to the nearest police station and there are also silent alarms which send a signal via the phone line to the police station without alerting the burglar so he can be caught in the act.

Burglar alarms are increasingly popular. The

NEVER AID THE BURGLAR

Nothing helps the potential burglar as much as clear indications that you are not at home and indeed that you may be away for some time.

• If you pop out for 20 minutes do not leave a helpful note saying so on the front door for your friend or the delivery man — you will be telling potential burglars as well.

• If you are going away, cancel the milk and papers in person, discreetly; there is no need to tell the whole street. Again, do not leave a note for just anyone to read.

• Ask a friend to come in every day and clear away mail and open and shut curtains, perhaps when they feed the cat. They might also turn lights on and off night and morning.

Even if the burglar knows that you are absent, you do not have to make it even easier for him by leaving him an unlocked shed or garage, perhaps full of useful tools or ladders. (An open, careless garage also advertises the fact that you are not there.) Finally, do not help him by leaving a window open for the cat to use; it is just asking for trouble.

People often unwittingly help the burglar by being careless about their house keys. Don't!

• Never leave a key in the lock on the inside of a door. If you do, a burglar may be able to turn it from the outside with a pair of tweezers or make a small hole in the door near the lock and use it to turn the key.

• Do not leave keys 'hidden' on string behind the letterbox, under a flowerpot or doormat or on top of the door frame. Everyone chooses the same sort of hiding place, even if it is not as obvious as these, and burglars no doubt get used to working out where they are.

• When you move into a new flat or house it is worth changing the major locks on the outside doors. If you do not do this you have no way of knowing how many keys there are in circulation or who has them.

• Do not label keys and avoid carrying them together with identification. Even if a lost key is returned, it may have been copied first. Change the relevant lock, getting a friend to stay in the house for you while you go out to buy one — and do not leave the house empty until you have finished the job of changing the lock.

████

most common types used are:

MAGNETIC ALARM SYSTEM With this system, magnetic contacts are attached to doors and windows and if these are opened, the electrical contact is broken, triggering the alarm. The system may also have contacts on internal doors and alarm-activating mats which work when trodden on.

INFRA-RED SYSTEM The infra-red rays create a barrier, say across a room or a doorway, and the alarm sounds when the barrier is broken by something or someone passing through it. There are also systems that use ultrasonic and radio waves in the same way.

PANIC BUTTON Most systems of whatever type can incorporate a panic button, perhaps at the bedside or by the front door. When pressed the button will trigger the alarm even when the rest of the system is turned off.

THE RIGHT SYSTEM There are several DIY alarm systems available in kit form; they are not difficult to fit but choose carefully as many are adequate to cover only a very small house. You may feel happier with a professional job but employ someone reputable or recommended to you – *not* a door-to-door convasser.

Whichever type you decide on, try to choose a system that will suit your particular home and habits: if you have a child who swaps bedrooms at night or an elderly relative who likes a midnight cup of tea, do not fit sensors inside the house. If that other burglar deterrent, your dog, is allowed free range of the place at night, do not put down alarm-activating pressure pads for him to set off.

Alarm systems vary a lot in price; unfortunately the more sophisticated and dependable a system is, the more expensive it will generally be. If you do not want to go for a complete system you might be interested in a single alarm.

SINGLE ALARM You can position one of these to protect just your front hall, for instance. A battery-operated control box is fixed to the wall by the front door and wired up so that the alarm covers adjacent doors and windows. Some have a panic button on the box as well.

DOOR CHAIN ALARM A good idea for a vulnerable

door or set of French windows, these are door chains incorporating an alarm and are fixed in the same way as an ordinary door chain. If the chain is removed from its slot, the alarm sounds.

FIRE HAZARDS

SOME COMMON CAUSES OF FIRE IN THE HOME

A fire in the home can be a frightening experience. Even when no one is hurt and little real damage is done, the shock can be severe and, afterwards, reminders in the form of an unpleasant, smoky smell and possible staining or other water damage can linger on for quite a while. Make fire prevention a priority.

COOKING OIL AND FAT Smoking hot fat or oil is so dangerous that it probably causes more kitchen fires than anything else. It does not merely catch fire if spilt or allowed to boil over, it can light spontaneously if overheated.

Chip pans are the main offenders. Never leave one unattended; do not overfill (the pan should never be more than two-thirds full *with* chips in), and make sure the chips (or whatever you are deep-frying) are dry before you put them in or the water will boil up angrily in the oil.

Should the pan catch fire, turn off the heat. Do *not* pour on water, do *not* open a door or window and do *not* try to carry the pan outside – the draught of air will make the fire worse. Extinguish the flames with the lid of the pan or a Pyrex plate or a fire blanket; the fire will go out if you deprive it of air. Leave the pan to cool before you remove the cover.

In the same way, should a fire break out in the oven, do not open the door but just turn off the heat and the fire will soon go out through lack of air. As an extra precaution with a gas oven, turn off the mains gas supply until the fire is out.

FIRES AND HEATERS Another common cause of fire, often involving a child, is still, even in the days of central heating, the open fire or oil or paraffin heater.

If you have an oil or paraffin heater, observe the following rules to reduce the risk of fire:

- Never try to fill it when it is already lit.
- If possible, take the heater to the source of fuel rather than vice versa, to avoid unnecessary spills inside the house.
- Do not move the heater when it is alight and do not place it in a draughty spot.
- Have the heater serviced regularly and buy from a reputable source – faulty heaters kill.

If the heater does begin to burn, pour on water if it stands on carpet; smother with a fire blanket or wet towel if not.

Never dry teatowels on or near your heater or on the front of the oven. Igniting teacloths and hand towels are an extremely common cause of fire in the kitchen.

An open fire requires a different set of safety rules, including a fireguard sufficient to prevent burning wood or coal tumbling on to the carpet. Put it in place whenever you leave the room, in case you are away longer than you had planned.

However, the prime fire precaution with an open fire must be to have the chimney swept regularly so that it is kept clear of soot and debris that might ignite. Smokeless fuels do not produce a lot of carbon deposits but if you burn coal or wood, a residue quickly builds up inside the chimney flue. If you have a fire every day, have the chimney swept after about three months, then again at the end of the winter ready for the first cold snap of autumn.

The flues and chimneys used by gas and other fuel-burning appliances also require regular sweeping. Like cooking oil fires, chimney fires are a frequent reason for the fire brigade being summoned.

If the chimney is on fire (often all you can see is smoke from *outside* the house and a neighbour may warn you), keep watch at an open hearth in case burning material falls down – scoop it up with a metal shovel – while you wait for the firemen to arrive.

CIGARETTES A cigarette left in an ashtray on the arm of a soft chair may result in no more than a bad burn on the cover but it can cause deaths if the upholstery ignites and the whole house goes up. Cigarette smoking in bed also causes many accidents as the smoker falls asleep and the bed-clothes catch fire; many of these fires are fatal.

Do not be casual about cigarettes (or matches). Make sure they are well stubbed out before you abandon them in an ashtray; do not put them in the rubbish bin until they are cold and do not balance them on the edge of an ashtray from where they might topple as they burn down.

FOAM-FILLED FURNITURE New fire safety regulations have recently been introduced to deal with the serious problem of foam-filled upholstered furniture catching light and giving off deadly toxic fumes as it burns. Unfortunately, because foam is a petroleum-based product, comprising 90 per cent air, it tends to ignite easily, reaching very high temperatures. Toxic fumes and thick black smoke are emitted, and oxygen in the air is quickly used up to be replaced by fatal carbon dioxide which causes death almost instantly.

The new regulations require that all foam supplied to manufacturers for use in upholstery and furnishings must now be of the Combustion Modified (CM) type. All furniture and furnishings sold through commercial retailers must contain only flame-retardant fillings which also give off less toxic fumes when they do burn, and be clearly labelled to this effect.

By March 1993 the regulations will also apply to secondhand furniture, except for that manufactured before 1950. In addition, all covering fabrics for sale, either permanent or loose covers, must meet and pass the match test. If the fabric cannot be flame-retardant treated, then a flame-retardant interliner or barrier fabric must be fitted immediately beneath it.

NOTE: If you plan to buy second-hand furniture privately, remember to be aware of possible safety hazards.

ELECTRICITY AS A FIRE HAZARD

Always treat electrical appliances and wiring with respect, keep them in good repair and do not forget basic safety requirements, usually printed on the labels of electrical products.

PLUGS Wire up correctly and always connect up the earth core of flex if there is one. Always use the cable grip when wiring a plug. Many people 'save time' by not fitting the flex through this but it can mean that the wires pull out from their terminals and then they may touch and short, possibly causing fire.

Fit the right fuse for the appliance to which the plug is attached: a red 3 amp fuse for items up to 700 watts and a brown 13 amp fuse for those over, including colour televisions, kettles, irons and washing machines.

The fuse serves as a safety device, a cut-out, if an appliance is overheating, so if you put in too strong a fuse it will not 'blow' and cut the electric current. Before you replace a fuse, check the appliance to see if all is well. It may just be that the fuse needs replacing but if it happens again, unless there is a fault in the electric circuit, the appliance probably needs attention.

ELECTRIC FLEX Use a flex of the correct weight for the appliance. Use two-core flex only for double-insulated appliances and for light fittings with no metal parts; all other appliances should be connected up to the earth.

Do not run leads across the floor or under the carpet where constant treading may damage the flex and cause shorting. If the flex is damaged at all, for instance cut, burned or worn through, do not just tape over the weakness (or worse, wind the bare wires together then cover with tape). For safety's sake, it may be necessary to make a *temporary* repair, but you must then either replace the whole lead (in the case of a small portable appliance), or fit a one-piece flex connector (in the case of a fixture, such as a stereo).

MULTIPLE ADAPTORS Do not plug too many appliances into any one socket by over-using a multiple adaptor – although how many is safe does depend on what you are plugging in. Never plug in more than one high-rated appliance; that is, anything with a heating element (e.g. electric fire, kettle, washing machine). Overloading leads to overheating leads to fire. Never use more than one socket adaptor in any one socket; to do so can cause sparking.

ELECTRIC BLANKETS Always make sure that an electric blanket is lying flat and smooth on the bed. Creases in it could cause the element to break. Never fold it to put it away for the summer; instead roll it up or keep it flat on a spare bed when not in use.

When the blanket is switched on, do not leave heavy objects such as a suitcase on the bed as this could cause the wire to overheat.

OVERHEATING

- Use a bulb of the correct wattage for the lampshade it is to be used with or the lampshade may burn. Lampshades are usually marked with the maximum wattage suitable.
- Never cover the air vents of appliances such as fridges and freezers and give them their full clearance at the back.
- Check at intervals that the thermostat is working properly on the immersion heater (you can probably get an idea from the heat of the water in the tap if it is doing its job); overheating here can have serious consequences.

TELEVISIONS Remove the aerial lead from the television if there is a thunder storm – this is because it is possible for lightning to be attracted down the aerial into the set.

GAS AS A FIRE HAZARD

Even greater care has to be taken when dealing with gas. Electrical faults may lead to an (initially anyway) localized fire, whereas a gas leak can end with an explosion. Now that non-poisonous natural gas is used, this is the prime worry with gas, apart from the danger of carbon monoxide from faulty or badly fitted heaters.

For safety reasons, gas appliances must always be installed either by the Gas Board or by a firm belonging to CORGI (the Confederation for the Registration of Gas Installers) and there are strict rules about gas safety. For instance, if you use or allow anyone else to use a faulty gas appliance or if it is in a room without proper ventilation, then you are legally responsible for any accident.

All gas appliances should therefore be serviced regularly and professionally repaired. If you are considering buying a secondhand gas fire or cooker, remember that you should have it checked by a qualified engineer, to satisfy the Gas Board as well as for your own peace of mind. You ought therefore to add the cost of this on to the price of the item when you are deciding whether or not to buy it.

GAS LEAK

The Gas Board have an obligation to run a 24-hour, 365-day emergency service to deal with gas escapes. Their telephone number should be in the telephone book under Gas; phone them at once if you are worried.

IF YOU SMELL GAS:

- Check that no gas cooker taps have been left on, unlit; that no pilot light has blown out any-where; and that the gas fire tap is not turned on. If something like this has happened, turn off any tap you find turned on and open the window to let the build-up of gas clear before you re-light the pilot light (or indeed light anything).

Until you know what the problem is:
- Extinguish all flames, including cigarettes.
- Don't strike a match.
- Turn off any gas taps that are on.
- Don't use any electric switches at all, not even the light or the doorbell as they may cause a spark, which could then ignite the gas.

IF YOU THINK IT IS A LEAK:

Turn off the whole gas supply at the main tap, usually by the meter, and call the Gas Board at once. Checking for suspected gas escape and simple gas escape repairs are usually free as there is no charge for the first half-hour or parts and materials under the cost of £1. If the work takes longer, you will be charged. There is no charge, however, if the leak is on their side of the main supply tap.

After the gas leak has been tracked down and dealt with, and when the gas supply goes back on, do not forget to relight the pilot lights.

FIRE FIGHTING

Do not try to tackle a fire yourself unless it has only just started and then only if you are confident you can deal with it alone.

FIRE EXTINGUISHERS Small extinguishers for domestic use have only a limited capacity, so keep them close at hand so you can stop a fire before it takes hold. The kitchen is probably the best place (with another in the garage if you have one). They are of three sorts: red water extinguishers (which are not suitable for electrical, fat or oil fires); blue dry-powder extinguishers (suitable for all fires, particularly those involving electricity, oil and fat); and vaporizing-liquid green ones which can be used on any small fires, particularly electrical ones.

FIRE BLANKET In the kitchen, also keep a safety blanket made of woven glass fibres which can be used to smother a small fire before it has a chance to get going. Keep it near the cooker to put out fires involving fat and/or electricity, then you will not be tempted to put water on the flames which would only make matters worse.

FIRE AND SMOKE DETECTORS In fact most people who die in (or after) fires die from asphyxia from smoke rather than from flames. Fit a smoke detector to the hall ceiling; this will let off a shrill alarm as soon as smoke reaches it and alert you in time to get out of the house, sometimes even before there are any flames. At night, a smoke detector will prevent you becoming unconscious from smoke and possibly toxic fumes before you even wake up or smell the fire.

There are two main types of fire detector on the market:

HEAT DETECTORS warn of fire by reacting to increasing heat.

SMOKE DETECTORS react to smoke and fumes drifting from the fire. Smoke detectors will usually give earlier warning of most fires and are therefore more suitable for use in the home. You can choose either an optical detector, which responds more quickly to smouldering fires, or an ionization model, which tends to react a little faster to flaming fires. (Some detectors do combine both devices but make sure they are connected so that only one of the mechanisms needs to be triggered before the alarm goes off.)

Most DIY outlets now sell battery-operated smoke alarms that are easily fitted by the householder. Models powered from the mains electrical supply are also available and should be fitted by a competent electrician. The most reliable method is a mains-operated model with a standby battery should the mains supply fail (look for BS number 5446 and the kitemark).

The best place to position a smoke detector depends on the size and layout of your home and where you and your family sleep. The most critical requirement for the positioning of a *single* detector is to choose a spot between the sleeping area(s) and the most likely sources of fire (living room or kitchen). But it should not be more than about ten paces (7 metres) from the door to any room where a fire might start and block your escape from the house. Your local fire brigade will be glad to offer further help and advice.

WHEN THERE IS A FIRE

FOR A SMALL FIRE, shut the door and windows of the room and use water on it unless it involves electricity or oil. If any electrical appliances are involved, unplug or switch them off at the mains before taking action. For these use a heavy rug, blanket or even your coat to smother the fire. (Use these also if a person's clothes are alight or roll the victim on the ground to smother the flames.) If you cannot put out the fire immediately, call the fire brigade and close the door on the fire.

IF THE FIRE SPREADS after you have closed the door and called the fire brigade, you must get everyone out of the house at once, just in case. Join them outside and stay there; don't go back in or you may get trapped.

IF YOU ARE TRAPPED in the house, close the door of the room and block it with a rug, bedding, towels, or whatever is available, to keep out the smoke. Go to the window and shout for help. If smoke gets into the room, lean out of the window to breathe or lie on the floor, where there will be less smoke than elsewhere.

Never jump from a window; drop by your hands from the windowsill if you have to. If you are in a bedroom, try to make some sort of escape rope by tying sheets to the bed or other heavy piece of furniture and pulling this across to the window in case you cannot afford to wait any longer for the fire brigade.

NOTE

Teach your children the dangers of fire and respect for its power. Without giving them nightmares, talk to them about what do if there is a fire – how to put blankets over doors, where to find window keys, when to lie on the floor, and the need to shout from windows, that sort of thing; if even one such scrap of information remains with them it might one day save a life.

PERSONAL SAFETY

Personal safety in the home is as much to do with your attitude and careful habits as with clever gadgets and elaborate safety equipment. Every home carries its own, if different, risks.

Think safe on behalf of the whole family and its visitors, from crawling babies to those whose eyesight and footing is perhaps not what it was. Without getting neurotic about it, always think ahead to possible dangers and accidents. When you put a glass too near the edge of a table, think again and move it, just in case someone's elbow catches it, causing it to shatter on the floor, a danger to anyone walking barefoot.

In the same way, make a habit of always running the cold water in the bath first in case you are called away for a moment. Your toddler might get bored with waiting and climb in on her own, and if the water is hot nasty scalds could result. (Running the cold first also helps to prevent condensation.) If you have to answer the door or the telephone, always take your toddler with you. A child can drown in a tiny amount of water.

Never put something down 'just for a minute' in a potentially unsafe place.

Dispose of razor blades thoughtfully in case, later in the week, you have to return to the bin to retrieve something you threw away by mistake – and cut yourself. Also, for the sake of the refuse collectors, wrap broken glass in a thick layer of newspaper before putting it in the bin or put it out separately, marked 'broken glass'.

Tidy away DIY equipment when you are not using it – screwdrivers, chisels and particularly electric drills can lead to bad injuries in the wrong hands, perhaps while being used as swords, daggers or guns!

In the kitchen, when you carry a hot pan across the room, always be aware that if there is someone else at home he or she might well pick that very moment to run into the room to tell you something, or to get something from the fridge. Also, if you are cooking and you have to leave what you are doing, turn the heat down or off, put the pan to one side, or take the pie out of the oven *before* you go to the door, or the 'phone. You may be held up talking so that you forget the cooking, or perhaps you simply cannot return for a short while.

Try to explain the reasons for your safety do's and don'ts to the rest of the household.

ELECTRICITY AND SAFETY

Electricity can kill: never attempt any electrical job unless you are sure you know what you are doing. Turn off the mains supply before you begin, or at least turn off and unplug the appliance you are working on. Make sure everyone of a suitable age knows where the mains on/off switch is, in case of accidents.

Water conducts electricity very efficiently. Never touch any electrical appliance or fitting with wet hands or use electric equipment in wet conditions, in particular out of doors. Never take portable appliances such as radios or hairdryers into the bathroom on an extension lead; the availability of electricity in the bathroom is limited deliberately to pull-cord light and wall heater fittings and isolated shaver points, for your safety.

Switch off all appliances before cleaning them, even if you are just trying to remove a piece of toast that is stuck in the toaster. Never attempt to poke about inside a live appliance for whatever reason, even if you are using a non-conductive material such as a (dry) wooden spoon.

Teach older children about the dangers of electricity and protect younger ones from them. The biggest danger areas are socket outlets and trailing flexes of all sorts. To avoid little fingers or, worse, metal objects being poked in, fit outlets with shuttered sockets or use the plastic safety covers that plug into the socket while you are not using it (these are cheap and widely available).

Try to position appliances and their flexes to avoid trailing so that they do not get tugged or tripped over. Turn the kettle so that it faces away from you; put the table lamp at the back not the front of the table; tuck away 'chewable' electrical leads under carpet and run them round the edge of rooms.

ELECTRICAL IMPORTS Many other countries have different, sometimes lower, standards when it comes to electrical safety; be aware of this when you buy imported goods or bring something back from your holiday. If in doubt, have them checked by a qualified electrician before using.

SAFETY IN THE GARDEN

PATHS AND STEPS When laying out a garden, do not make it into an obstacle course, with paths jumping from one direction to another. Never run a narrow path right alongside a pond; it might make an elderly person nervous and would be an invitation to a small child to step too close to the edge.

Paths and steps covered in moss and lichen can be dangerous. Remove as much growth as possible with a spade, then wash down using a proprietary moss killer or a solution of about 1 eggcup of bleach to each bucket of warm water.

PONDS A little child can drown in only a few centimetres of water. A garden pond, however small or shallow, always presents a danger. For peace of mind, it is worth draining the pool until the children are older. Alternatively, strong wire netting should be used to cover the pool completely, firmly secured with pegs in the ground.

SOME POISONOUS PLANTS TO LOOK OUT FOR:

Broom: the seeds are poisonous but it is not likely to be serious unless eaten in quantity.

Castor oil plant: the plant and seeds are very poisonous – six seeds are fatal for a child.

Cypress spurge: the oil in the seeds has a purgative effect; the milky sap can cause blistering to the skin and, internally, burning.

Deadly nightshade: the very pretty berries are very poisonous (woody nightshade slightly less so).

Foxglove: all parts are poisonous, especially the leaves.

French bean: the raw beans are dangerous if more than a few are eaten.

Greater celandine (and buttercup): cases of poisoning in humans are very rare.

Guelder rose: beware of chewing or eating the fruit, bark or leaves.

Henbane: all parts of the plant are poisonous.

Holly: you would have to eat 20 to 30 berries before it was fatal but you could have a bad tummy-ache.

Honeysuckle: some types are poisonous.

Horse chestnut: eating the unripe fruits and green capsules could make you very ill.

Ivy: the stem, leaves and berries are all poisonous but the berries are so bitter that there is little temptation.

Laburnum: the flowers, seeds and roots are all poisonous.

Lupin: it is the lupin seeds that can be dangerous, as they look like peas.

Mezereon (Daphne): all parts of the plant are dangerous, including the shoots and berries; it can also cause inflammation and blistering on the skin.

Mistletoe: the leaves and fruit are poisonous.

Privet: the berries are poisonous.

Rowan: eating lots of raw rowan berries can be dangerous (but they are safe when cooked).

Runner beans: a large number of raw beans could kill a child.

Snowberry: the very pretty berries are poisonous.

Yew: it is not the red berries but the needles and twigs of the yew that are poisonous so, though animals are at risk, a child is unlikely to be hurt by this plant.

FENCING AND GATES Likewise, if you make sure that all fencing/hedges/walls are sound and secure, with no way for a child to get out, you will be able to relax. Do not forget that a determined baby can crawl through quite a small hole or thin patch in a hedge.

Have a self-closing gate and fit it with an extra childproof catch if this seems to be necessary. Check that the gate is closed and the catch on every time you use the garden.

SHEDS The natural home for all those unpleasant weedkillers, slug baits and rat poisons, to say nothing of greenfly spray and even fertilizer, the garden shed can be a death-trap. Weed and vermin killers are frequently poisonous and could make a child seriously ill, so always keep them safely locked up and well out of reach.

Store any DIY equipment with safety in mind as well, including garden tools such as secateurs that could easily take off a small finger.

CLIMBING FRAMES Inspect metal frames regularly for rust spots, sharp corners and loose bolts, then treat and repair as necessary. Check wooden frames for rot and treat accordingly.

PLANTS Quite a few garden plants (and some house plants too) are poisonous and if you have small children it is a good idea to avoid these because of children's fondness for eating pods and berries that look rather like familiar fruits and vegetables. For instance, just three or four laburnum pods can be lethal for a child, as can 10 or 12 red mezereon berries. Not all of the parts of plants that are poisonous are attractive to eat – for example yew needles, the very bitter berries of ivy, and the unripe fruits and green capsules of the horse chestnut.

Children are not always good at remembering which growing things are safe to eat and which are not, so to be on the safe side, tell them not to eat anything that is growing.

IN THE KITCHEN

The average kitchen is a very busy place, full of boiling liquids, hot surfaces and sharp edges, and it is no wonder that so many domestic accidents happen there. Many of them could be avoided.

The first step is to plan the kitchen properly: so that people do not use the working part of the kitchen as a passage through to cloakroom or garden. You should also plan so that you do not find yourself regularly lifting down heavy pans from above shoulder height (either use a steady pair of steps, kept nearby to make sure that you do use them, or reorganize your storage arrangements). Make sure that you never have to carry hot pans across the room, especially across a doorway, to get to the sink or work surface (and you should always have a safe hot-resting place for such next to the cooker). Have blinds, not curtains near a stove. If possible, do not place the cooker below a window. Someone may get burned reaching up to open or close it and the draught may blow out a gas pilot light, leading to a potentially dangerous situation.

The second step is to use the kitchen safely: wipe up spills at once to avoid slips and falls. Always keep knives sharp; a blunt knife is more likely to slip and because you have been putting more pressure on it, it is more likely to cut you when it does slip. Store knives on a wall rack or in a special stand where children cannot reach them, not in a drawer where you might cut yourself if you are not looking (and the knife edges will be damaged). When there are children around, fit a cooker guard or at least keep all pans on the back burners when you are not actually standing over them so that children will not be tempted to reach up to the handles. If possible, fit a safety gate to keep tiny children out of the room altogether or put them in a play-pen so they are at least out of the working area.

Finally, take care to maintain and redecorate with safety in mind. Choose a non-slip type of flooring and avoid small mats that might trip you up. Fit and use a good lighting system, either overall fluorescent or local directed spotlights. You cannot work safely in the gloom. Never have polystyrene ceiling tiles above the cooker in case of a pan fire. Keep the cooker hood clean and free of greasy build-up; dirt and grease make the hood less effective, as well as increasing the risk of fire.

POISONS

Poisoning is all too common in the home. Children are the main, but not the only, sufferers and not all of the guilty products would be immediately recognized as poisons.

DIY preparations have become very sophisticated and therefore potentially dangerous in recent years. Do not take risks: read through the instructions fully before starting to use them.

Also, many products, particularly cleaning fluids, give off harmful fumes. The effect is often cumulative, that is, the substance enters the body and is not dispersed, so that each small exposure to the chemical adds up to what can, in some cases, be a lethal dose. So, before using anything that gives off fumes or vapours or smells strongly or has a warning on the packet, open all the windows in a room, then try to avoid breathing the fumes directly. (Never mix two chemicals together unless you know what you are doing; poisonous fumes often result.)

Manufacturers are not always obliged by law to declare that their products are poisonous. For example, carpet cleaners, disinfectants, dyes, lavatory cleaners, perfumes and white spirit all are, or contain, poisons. They are all safe if used correctly but should be kept out of the reach of young children – under the sink or in the understairs cupboard will not do (remember, too, that many of these poisons are highly flammable and a flare-up under the stairs is the last thing you want when trying to escape from a fire).

LEAD Most paint is now lead-free (check when you buy) but paint with a lead base is still on the woodwork in some houses and on old painted furniture. If you have a baby, repaint any suspect item that a child might suck, such as the arm of a wooden chair or a cot side. If your child likes to have a bite at it as well, remove the old paint first, but do not use heat as this may create dangerous lead fumes.

MEDICINES Keep a close check on all medicines; what does you good will probably harm a child, especially if taken in quantity as 'sweets'. It is unfortunate that the manufacturers persist in making pills that look so appealing to a child.

And it is not just a matter of preventing children from poisoning themselves. It is easy to make a mistake yourself, so read the dosage instructions carefully and follow them precisely; never give or take medicines in the dark.

Throw old or left-over medicine down the drain and dissolve old pills or flush them down the lavatory. You can also sometimes return them to the chemist for safe disposal.

HALL, STAIRS AND FLOORS

Keep the floors clear and do not let briefcases and sports bags pile up in the hallway, together with out-of-season coats or jackets and boxes waiting for the next jumble sale. Do not block the hall with bicycles or prams either. Apart from the constant irritation these things cause, you may need a clear run to the front door (or round to the back) if a fire should break out.

Never leave objects of any sort on the stairs. Toys tend to be the worst offenders: tiny things like marbles and Lego bricks can easily cause you to lose your footing, while skates and balls can be just as dangerous, though not as funny as they are in cartoons. One aid that can save you if you do stumble is a firm hand-rail; you should have such a rail on at least one side of the staircase.

Good lighting is essential in areas of much heavy traffic. For the stairs, angle this from the side and avoid variation in the lighting. Fit a two-way switch so that you can turn on the lighting whether you are at the top or bottom of the stairs. A switch with an integral 'eye' sensitive to light that will turn on the lighting when the natural light lessens is a good idea for stairways.

The heavy traffic in hall and stairway not only wears out the flooring but demands that it be replaced. These are the last places where you can afford to have tears and holes in carpet or sheet flooring. (On the stairs carpet should be laid so that it continues beyond the top step, to avoid anyone tripping up where it begins.)

Insecurely fixed carpet is also a safety hazard, especially on the stairs, where it can cause a serious accident. Replace worn or insecure carpet if at all possible or remove or fix it.

FIRST AID

What is First Aid?

First aid is the immediate treatment given to a casualty for any injury or sudden onset of illness. The aims of first aid are to keep the injured person alive, to relieve suffering, to prevent further injury, and finally to hand him or her over without delay for expert medical attention. The following information gives you the basics but it will help if you go on a recognized first aid course as well.

Basic Rules

When you are faced with serious injury or illness follow the first aid ABC to ensure that the casualty's primary needs are provided for:

- an open Airway
- adequate Breathing
- proper Circulation.

Whatever other problems may be present, for life to continue oxygen must be able to get into the lungs so that this can then be spread around the body in the blood. While parts of the body can survive some while without oxygen, others, most importantly nerve cells in the brain, will be damaged very quickly, after as little as three minutes without oxygen. If the blood is not carrying enough oxygen the person will look blue, especially in the lips, earlobes and nails.

OPEN THE AIRWAY

Take action at once if you suspect that either an obstruction and/or unconsciousness is preventing air getting freely into the lungs. For instance, vomit may lie at the back of the throat, blocking the airway, or the casualty's tongue may loll across it during unconsciousness.

● Loosen any restrictive clothing at the throat, chest or waist.

● Lift the chin up with one hand while pressing the forehead back with the other so that the jaw lifts the tongue clear (the nostrils should now be pointing upwards). Support the lower jaw so that the teeth are closed.

Breathing may restart naturally at this point. If not, or if the breathing is noisy, look for an obstruction in the mouth.

● Hook in two fingers and clear out any food or broken teeth or dentures. Use a handkerchief to clean out blood or vomit. Do not push anything into the throat while doing so.

ARTIFICIAL RESPIRATION

If an ill or injured person is not breathing, it is sometimes possible to start the breathing again by 'breathing' for him yourself, passing air directly from your lungs to his by blowing. As the body needs constant oxygen, you must begin artificial breathing (respiration) as soon as you discover that a casualty is not breathing; re-establishing natural breathing takes priority over any other problems.

CHILDREN For children, use the same technique as for adults (shown on pages 122-23) but slightly faster and not so hard.

For the under twos, open the airway as described for adults, but do not tilt the head too far back. Seal both mouth and nose with your mouth and puff air in gently at a rate of about 20 breaths a minute. After the first couple of inflations check for a heart beat: feel for a pulse on the inside of the upper arm.

For the over twos, seal your mouth around either mouth and nose or the mouth or nose only, depending on the size of the child, and puff in as for under twos.

ARTIFICIAL RESPIRATION

For artificial respiration, proper training is really necessary, though should you find yourself with no alternative, then the information

ADULTS

• Lie the casualty on his back and tilt back his head while supporting the back of his neck with the other hand. Keep the chin up and blow air deeply and slowly into either the mouth or the nose (sealing the other to prevent air escaping) until the chest rises, showing that you have inflated the lungs. If the chest fails to rise, check that you have the casualty's head in the correct position (see page 121); if it still does not rise after this, check for an obstruction in the airway.
• Remove your mouth and allow the air to escape from the lungs – watch the chest fall.
• Repeat. If the heart is beating, the effect of the first few inflations should be a change in the casualty's colour from a blue/grey pallor towards pinkness. Give the first six to ten inflations fairly promptly, one after the other, then work according to the reaction of your casualty. If he is pinkish, he is probably getting enough oxygen so just keep going steadily; if he is still pale blue/grey, he is not getting an adequate supply of oxygen, so try to get more air into him more quickly. But always wait for all the air to escape before you blow in again.
• If the casualty begins to breathe again himself, let your inflations coincide with his own breathing in, and continue until you feel that he can cope alone. It can seem hopeless to go on with artificial respiration but persistence is sometimes rewarded, even after as long as an hour, so keep going (as long as the heart is beating).
• When the casualty is breathing naturally, place him in the recovery position and watch to make sure that breathing continues.

here will point the way for you. Never practise on a person breathing normally.

Tilt back the head to clear the airway.

Blow a firm, deep breath into the mouth.

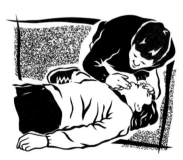

Check to see that the chest has risen.

THE RECOVERY POSITION

This means lying face downwards but with the head turned to one side and with the arm and leg on that side pulled up to prevent the casualty from flopping down completely on his front. The chin should also be pulled up to keep the airway clear.

If possible the recovery position should also include the casualty lying slightly head-downwards so that any fluids can drain freely from his mouth. Never give a pillow; this has quite the opposite effect.

You may have to modify this position if bones are broken or space is limited. If you understand the reasoning behind it, however, you should be able to do this safely. (Lying the casualty face downwards with a rolled blanket under one side of his body can be helpful.) Proceed with caution if you suspect a spinal injury; in these circumstances it is essential to keep the spine straight.

MAINTAINING THE CIRCULATION

However efficient your artificial respiration, the effort is wasted unless the heart is beating and circulating the oxygen in the blood.

Check for circulation by feeling the carotid pulse at the neck, between the voice box and the adjoining muscle. In a small child check the brachial pulse, inside the upper arm – press gently against the bone of the arm.

A non-beating heart can sometimes be stimulated into action by using the technique of external chest compression, which involves pressing down at regular intervals on the lower half of the breastbone (between the ribs). This increases

---

External chest compression is a precise technique that requires practical experience and should not be attempted by the untrained. An experienced person can use it together with artificial respiration but, unlike artificial respiration, external chest compression should never be used to support the natural action of the heart as this can be easily upset. So this technique should never be used if the heart is beating on its own, however faint the heartbeat may be.

the pressure inside the chest and forces blood out of the heart and into the arteries, then as the pressure is relieved blood flows back along the veins, refilling the heart as it expands again. This is *not* a technique to be used by the untrained – see the note in the box on page 124.

CONTROLLING BLOOD LOSS

Obviously, stopping blood loss after an injury is vital to maintaining the circulation. Do this by using pressure on the wound and by raising the injured part of the body, if possible, to slow down the flow of blood to the area.

If you are certain that there are no foreign bodies in the wound, press directly on the wound for up to 15 minutes to halt the flow of blood and give it a chance to clot. It will help if you can keep the casualty still.

Use a dressing pad, sterile if possible, if one is available – but even a clean teatowel or wad of tissues will do – and hold it against the wound. If you secure it in place, do so firmly but not so tightly as to cut off the circulation. If bleeding comes through, put more padding or bandaging over the original; do not disturb the clotting process by removing it.

If no dressing is available, use your hands: hold together the edges of any gaping wound by squeezing gently.

If you suspect that there may be foreign material (glass, etc.) in the wound, press near the wound rather than directly over it.

COPING IN AN EMERGENCY

The ability to keep calm in an emergency, whether it is caused by illness or injury, is probably your most valuable asset. Do not panic and use your common-sense to do the best you can in the circumstances. Do not attempt too much: if you can stop someone's condition worsening and/or prevent other people from getting caught up in the situation, for instance after a road accident, you will have done well.

SAFETY

In the case of a road accident, put out a signal to warn following motorists of trouble or ask someone to direct traffic away from the spot. It is all too common for one such incident to set off a series of accidents, especially when traffic is travelling at speed or in the dark. Be aware of possible danger from fire: there is always a risk where petrol is spilled. Turn off the ignitions of all involved vehicles. Remove casualties from the immediate area if possible.

If you find someone suffering from the effects of gas, poisonous fumes or fire, act quickly to remove him from any further danger before attempting treatment. If you cannot remove him, turn off any supply taps available and ventilate the room. Never plunge into a burning house; wait for the fire brigade. If the casualty is electrocuted and still in contact with the source of the electricity, turn this off or remove him with something that does not conduct electricity (use a wooden broom handle to push the casualty away from the source of the electricity). Do not touch him until contact with the current has been broken.

GETTING HELP

Once you have dealt with the casualty's most urgent needs (see rules ABC on page 120) phone for assistance; if there is someone else available, send them off immediately. Be as precise as possible in your description of where you are and what problems you have on your hands.

TREATING FOR SHOCK

Keep anyone showing signs of shock warm (but not hot), quiet and lying down until medical assistance arrives. Symptoms include: cold, damp, pale skin; feeling giddy or faint; shallow breathing and weak pulse; restlessness and gasping for air; thirst or sickness; unconsciousness.

Reassure and watch closely all casualties, including those suffering from shock, but *do not* give anything to eat or drink. If an anaesthetic should be necessary, recent intake of food or drink will cause a delay that might be dangerous.

HOW TO ADMINISTER FIRST AID

Luckily, most of the time our first aid is used to deal with ordinary everyday cuts and bruises, with only the occasional scare as a child threatens to choke on a piece of apple or has a nosebleed that will not stop. But it is just as important to use commonsense when dealing with these less dramatic incidents as it is in a major emergency.

Approach each situation calmly; children especially are easily panicked and any hurt person is slightly nervous and upset. It is up to you to reassure them the problem can be dealt with and if you cannot handle it yourself, the doctor can. If you show your fear and alarm it will only upset the casualty without doing any good at all.

If, for instance, you see a nasty cut on the forehead and are thinking 'Oh no! This is going to mean stitches and they hurt!' – just keep it to yourself; it may not even come to that. If you do have to say that something unpleasant of this sort may be necessary, present the fact in a sympathetic but matter-of-fact way. If the child is old enough to understand and wants to know, explain briefly what is involved rather than let a spectre of the unknown blow up in his or her mind to frightening proportions. Say, perhaps, how good anaesthetics are – the spray-on sort can mean no injection for example – and try to explain how the fear of 'having things done' to you is usually worse than the reality.

Do everything you can to relax the casualty; it will not only keep him or her happier, it can mean any treatment actually hurts less, as pain is less likely if the muscles are relaxed.

LET NATURE DO HER BIT

Do not go over the top in the way you treat minor ailments either. Sometimes good sterile dressings, stitches and painkillers *are* necessary but people are often too ready to rush for these where they are not essential. We must rely to a certain extent on our body's natural defences and *assist* them, by cleaning a cut well for instance.

FIRST-AID KIT

Every home, car or caravan should have a well-stocked first-aid kit. Store this in a clean, dry, air-tight container (such as a plastic box with a snap-on lid) and keep it somewhere dry – not in a steamy kitchen or bathroom for example – but near at hand. Mark it clearly and make sure that all adults and older children of the household know where it is kept.

The contents of your first-aid kit may vary: for instance you might want it to be more extensive if you were setting off on a camping holiday in remote countryside than if you were at home where useful items are close at hand. It should include cottonwool, various sizes of sterile dressing, a triangular bandage, safety pins, antiseptic, tweezers and scissors. Other items will depend on your own habits and requirements but, ideally, you would have available the following:

- Sterile dressings: small, medium and large
- Triangular bandages
- Cotton wool (and cotton buds)
- Roll of adhesive plaster
- Sterile gauze pads
- 5 cm (2 inch) and 7.5 cm (3 inch) wide cotton bandage
- 7.5 cm (3 inch) crepe bandage
- Assorted adhesive plaster dressings
- Safety pins and/or bandage clips
- Blunt-ended scissors
- Good tweezers
- Thermometer
- Eyebath
- Bowl for diluting antiseptic
- Liquid and cream antiseptic
- Paper tissues
- Mild painkillers such as paracetamol
- Paper and pencil is a good idea, especially if you are away from home, as is a torch.
- For a day out, when you do not want to carry a whole kit with you, pop into your bag a pocket pack of paper tissues, several individually wrapped antiseptic wipes and a couple of adhesive plasters.

A-Z OF FIRST AID

ACHES

Headaches or migraine Place a cold compress or wrapped hot water bottle on the sufferer's forehead and lie him down, preferably somewhere quiet and dark. Give a mild painkiller.

Be aware that a headache can be a sign of a more serious problem, especially when accompanied by other symptoms such as nausea, stiff neck or disturbed vision. Seek medical assistance if any of these symptoms are present or if the headache persists.

Toothache Until a visit to the dentist is possible, give mild painkillers or try a local treatment: soak a small piece of cottonwool in oil of cloves and ask the sufferer to bite on this with the affected tooth. Lying down with a hot water bottle to the cheek can also bring some relief.

Earache To ease the discomfort, give painkillers and have the sufferer rest with a hot water bottle. You may also drip a few drops of warmed oil (e.g. olive oil or sunflower oil) into the aching ear and plug with cottonwool. (To warm the oil, pour it into a teaspoon which you have warmed by dipping it into hot water before drying it.)

If pain continues or is accompanied by other problems, such as loss of balance or a discharge from the ear, seek a doctor's advice.

Stomach ache There is rarely need to worry about stomach ache alone unless it goes on for more than about half an hour; it is probably just indigestion or constipation. Let the patient rest quietly; if the ache is caused by menstrual cramps a hot water bottle may help. If there are additional symptoms such as vomiting or diarrhoea seek medical assistance.

BITES

Animal bites Because of the germs in the mouths of animals, any bite that breaks the skin should be well cleaned with cottonwool squeezed out in warm water or a weak antiseptic solution. For the treatment of serious bites where there is more of an injury see below under Wounds.

A tetanus injection may be thought necessary

if the person bitten is not already inoculated against this and if you are abroad the risk of rabies must be considered. Seek medical help and report the animal bite to the police.

Snake bites In this country the only wild snake that is poisonous is the adder; there are however others kept as pets. Although snake bites are rarely fatal it is very frightening to be bitten so be reassuring, and wash out the wound with soap and water. Keep the casualty still, with the bitten part, usually the arm or leg, below the level of the heart and call for an ambulance or transport to a hospital yourself.

For the appropriate anti-venom serum to be given, the doctor will need to identify the snake, so take note of its colour and markings, or if it is dead or in a secure container, take it with you.

BLISTERS Blisters are thin bubbles that form over skin that has been damaged by heat or by rubbing, as a result of fluid from the body tissue seeping into the area under the hurt skin. Once new skin has grown and the fluid has been re-absorbed, the blister has done its protective job. Do not burst a blister but assist it by protecting further with a plaster or other dressing; do not put anything adhesive on the blister itself.

BRUISING Bruises are caused by the blood from damaged blood vessels leaking into the sur-rounding tissue and are not on their own usually serious. Apply a cold compress (ice cubes in a plastic bag or even a pack of frozen peas) to slow down the flow of blood and reduce swelling. There are many folk remedies for treating bruis-ing – arnica, witch hazel, butter, even a paste of starch and water all have their supporters.

If you fear that the bruising may be more than superficial, see a doctor.

BURNS The main thing to remember with any burn, whether caused by fire, hot liquids (a scald) or chemicals, is to cool the injured part *at once* by plunging it into cold water, running or pouring cold water over it or laying on a cold compress. Even covering with wet towels or handkerchiefs will help. Continue with this for at least 15 minutes. After burning, the body tissues will otherwise go on 'cooking' for several minutes, increasing the damage already caused.

Remove any watches, rings or shoes in the burned area in case of swelling and cover the burn with a clean, preferably sterile, non-fluffy dressing. Whether or not you need to seek further assistance will depend on the spread and depth of the burn. If the burn still hurts after an hour, seek medical advice.

● Burns covering a wide area will typically vary in depth over their area. Do not apply any cream or ointment but cover with a pad of clean gauze or other fabric and seek medical attention at once.

● Small but deep burns like electric burns can be more dangerous than they seem. If there is any charring of the skin or if an ulcer develops within a few days, see a doctor.

Because of the damage done to the skin by burning there is a risk of infection entering the body. This is why clean, dry, preferably sterile dressings are important. Use non-fluffy fabric and make the dressing large enough to cover more than the actual burn area. For a burnt hand or a foot you can even use a clean plastic bag rather than leave it uncovered on the way to the hospital. Do not remove clothing or anything else that is sticking to a burn.

As a general rule, any burn that is larger than 2.5 cm (1 inch) in diameter should be seen by a doctor. The greater the proportion of the body a burn covers the more serious it is: what is a trivial burn to an adult may not be so to a child.

Burns can involve a great loss of fluid from the body. Give small drinks of water (half a cupful every 15 minutes) to help compensate for this.

CHOKING If food has 'gone down the wrong way' or a child has got something caught in his throat and coughing does not bring it up, slap him sharply on the back up to four times, between the shoulder blades. If the casualty is leaning forwards this helps; hold a small child upside down to slap, put a larger child head down over your knee. If this does not work, try to hook out the obstruction with a finger but be careful not to push it further down.

If slapping between the shoulder blades has been attempted twice without success, a trained first aider may also use the technique of abdominal thrust. This method forces air up out of the casualty's lungs, thus dislodging the obstruction, but it really does need practical experience as it can cause internal injury.

CONCUSSION A fall or a blow to the head – or to the jaw – can sometimes result in brain concussion, a temporary disturbance in the normal working of the brain. This usually happens after a loss of consciousness but someone who is concussed may not even remember that he *was* unconscious. The signs are pale, cold and clammy skin, shallow breathing and weak but rapid pulse while still unconscious and, afterwards, nausea and feeling dazed, loss of memory, headache. Children, who fall easily as they play, should be watched closely after a fall for signs of concussion. In reaction to the shock they will often fall asleep; this is quite normal. However, if they display signs of concussion while asleep or afterwards, seek medical advice at once. They may be taken into hospital for a short period of observation. Adults with these symptoms should also see a doctor. In the meantime watch their breathing and keep the airway clear.

CONVULSIONS Convulsions usually occur in young children as a result of a high temperature caused by an infection. The symptoms of convulsions include: looking flushed, twitching, stiffness and arching of the back, holding breath, eyes rolled up.

All that is necessary is to cool the child by removing clothing and sponging down with tepid water. Then put him in the recovery position and cover lightly. Seek medical aid.

Convulsions are rarely dangerous and are not related to epileptic fits.

CRAMP When cramp suddenly contracts the muscles in a leg, foot or hand it can be quite painful and disabling but it is easily put right. Straighten out the affected part and then massage gently to ease the muscles.

Calf With the leg out straight, flex the foot by turning upwards towards the shin.

Foot Straighten out the toes using your hand and then stand on the ball of the affected foot.

DROWNING In drowning, water prevents air from entering the lungs, so breathing stops. Do not waste time trying to clear water from the casualty's lungs but act at once. Do not even wait to get the casualty out of the water – only his head need be clear of it for you to begin artificial respiration (scc pages 121-23) – and after the first few inflations continue on dry land. If you are successful and breathing starts again, place the casualty in the recovery position and keep him warm. Take the casualty to hospital in case the lungs have been affected.

FAINTING This is usually caused by a reduction in the flow of blood to the brain because of such things as lack of food or air, fatigue, and standing still for a long time (for example where blood has collected in the lower part of the body and the legs of soldiers on parade). Some people also faint in reaction to fear or pain.

If a person feels faint – is unsteady, nauseous and sweating – advise him to sit down, put his head between his knees and take deep breaths. If he does faint, lie him in the recovery position. Loosen any tight clothing and make sure that he is getting enough air. Reassure him as he regains consciousness and check that there are no side-effects, for example from the fall as he fainted. Do not give alcohol, or indeed anything to drink, until he is fully conscious again.

FITS Once seen, always recognizable, epileptic fits can be frightening to bystanders as the epileptic, losing consciousness, falls, becomes rigid and sometimes blue in the face and then jerks around, sometimes frothing at the mouth. When the muscles relax the epileptic will become still.

All you can do is to try to prevent him from hurting himself as he falls, perhaps by easing him down to the ground gently. Loosen any tight clothing and when the convulsions have stopped, place the epileptic in the recovery position until the attack is over. Do not put anything between his teeth – as used to be advised – and never give anything to eat or drink until you are satisfied that he is fully alert again.

If you find someone unconscious or having a fit, look for a medic-alert card or bracelet that may give details of his or her condition.

FRACTURES Fractures are bones cracked or broken either by a direct blow, for example when a car bumper hits the leg, or indirectly, as when the forearm or collarbone breaks after a fall on to the hand.

There are two sort of fracture – closed and open (where the covering skin has been broken). Once any wound of this sort has been dealt with, possibly padded to protect any protruding bone ends (as for foreign bodies in wounds, page 140), treat both sorts of fractures in the same way until you can get to a hospital.

It is not always easy to tell whether a bone is fractured, or if it is just sprained or dislocated. The signs of fractures are: pain and tenderness in the area, swelling and bruising, inability to use a limb and unnatural movement within the limb or in the way it is lying. If in doubt, treat the injury as if it is a fracture.

On the whole, do not attempt to straighten fractured limbs; certainly do not do so forcibly. If it is necessary to bring a fractured limb into a straight position, to immobilize it for instance, do so slowly while pulling *very* gently on the casualty's hand or foot. Do not stop pulling until the limb is securely immobilized.

You need something firm to hold the broken bones in place; whenever possible use the rest of the body for this, for example by tying an injured leg to the uninjured one, or in the case of a fractured arm, bandaging that arm, above and below the fracture, to the main part of the body. Pad between the limb and body to lessen jarring.

To help keep a leg straight, tie both feet together at the ankles in a figure-of-eight round the ankles and feet. Where feet and/or ankles only are injured, raise and support them on cushions. If it is essential to move the casualty before a fracture has been satisfactorily immobilized, support the fractured part, then move as gently as possible to prevent pain and further damage.

Circulation The circulation can become restricted, either because of the fracture itself or simply because the bandaging is too tight, so keep a watch for danger signs: blue or white rather than pink fingers or toes, loss of feeling beyond the injured part, lack of pulse at wrist or ankle. Ask the casualty to say what he feels.

If the dressings are to blame, loosen them. Fractures of the elbow sometimes lead to problems with circulation, especially in children, because the artery that lies near that joint is at risk of being compressed if the arm is bent. Serious bleeding can also result if this artery is torn by the broken bone, so keep the arm straight in the case of a fractured elbow.

Forearm, wrist, hand and fingers Bend at the elbow so that the arm lies across the body and fit a sling to immobilize the arm.

Jaw Support a broken jaw with a pad under the chin and a bandage up over the head.

Spine If injury to the spine is suspected, do not move the casualty, even to put him into the recovery position, unless you can do so properly, keeping the spine straight. If in doubt, do not move at all unless other circumstances make it necessary. Wait for an ambulance and keep the injured person calm.

FOREIGN BODIES

Eye Grit is the most common problem and can usually be removed by blinking or with the end of a moistened handkerchief. Seat the patient facing the light so that you can see in the eye easily and, standing behind, get him to tilt his head back towards you, then look in all directions while you search the eye.

If the foreign body is under the upper lid, ask him to look down then draw the lid down and out over the lower lashes; this should free it. Alternatively, use an eye bath to immerse the eye in water so that it floats off. Discourage the patient from rubbing the eye. Never try to remove anything that is on the coloured part of the eye or anything that seems to be stuck on or in the eye. If the grit cannot be easily removed, cover the eye with a clean pad and go to hospital, preferably a specialist eye hospital if there is one near to you.

Ear and nose This problem usually involves a child and unless the object that has been pushed in can easily be taken hold of, seek medical help.

The nose and ear are delicate instruments and are easily damaged.

> **NOTE**
> Discharge from the nose, sometimes blood-stained, can be a sign that a bead or bean is there, even though the child may have completely forgotten about it.

By mouth If you suspect that someone has inhaled a foreign body that does not come out with coughing, take the patient to hospital for attention. (See also under Choking, pages 131-2.)

Swallowing foreign bodies is often a problem with small children, who love to put things in their mouth. To deal with choking, follow the advice above, but if a foreign body has gone right down, treatment will vary according to the object. A marble will probably go straight through without causing any problem. Check it *has* passed through and if you are in doubt, consult the doctor. On the other hand, if something sharp like an open safety pin is swallowed, take the child straight to hospital without giving anything to eat or drink.

HEART ATTACK The signs are a gripping pain in the chest which may extend down the arms, a weak and irregular pulse, pale, damp skin, shortness of breath and possibly loss of consciousness.

Reassure the casualty and let him rest in a half-sitting position with head and shoulders supported and knees bent – put a cushion under them. To help get oxygen into the brain loosen any constricting clothing around the throat, chest and waist. Send for an ambulance and while you wait check the pulse rate every five or every ten minutes and pass on this information to the ambulancemen. If the casualty becomes unconscious, but is breathing normally, put in the recovery position; if breathing fails, clear the airway and give artificial respiration.

HEATSTROKE This happens when the heat-regulating system of the body breaks down, so that the body cannot control its temperature by sweating. This may be as the result of a feverish illness or of unaccustomed heat and humidity.

The skin will be burning hot and dry, the pulse fast and strong. The patient may complain of a headache and dizziness and become confused or unconscious. Get the sufferer into the shade or somewhere cool. Sponge down with tepid water and fan until the temperature drops to 38°C (101°F). Call a doctor.

NOSEBLEED Bleeding from the nose is usually caused by a blow or simply by sneezing or blowing the nose hard. It can also occur suddenly in elderly people who suffer from high blood pressure. 'Watery' bleeding from the nose after a blow on the head can mean that the skull has been fractured; seek medical attention.

Sit the patient quietly, head bent forward (to prevent blood running back down the throat) with his fingers pinching the soft part of the nostrils together. After 10 minutes he may release his grip gently; if bleeding continues he should repeat this for a further 10 minutes, then repeat again if necessary.

While doing this the patient should breathe through the mouth and continue to do so afterwards, so as not to disturb the blood clot formed. He should avoid blowing his nose for some hours. Seek medical attention if bleeding continues for more than 30 minutes or if there are repeated bouts of bleeding.

POISONING If you think that someone – usually a child – has swallowed a poison, such as plant berries, pills or cleaning liquid, get him to hospital fast. For appropriate treatment the doctor will want to know what the poison is, so try to discover this and write down its name or take a sample with you; also take any container, as this may indicate just how much has been taken.

There is little you can do yourself but if any liquid remains around the mouth, wash it away with cold water. If the poison is something corrosive such as bleach or an acid, give sips of milk or water to dilute it and cool the lips and mouth but do not induce vomiting, as this may cause the throat and mouth to be burned again as the chemical comes up.

If the casualty is unconscious, clear the airway and place in the recovery position so that any vomit can escape (keep the vomit for identification purposes). If it is necessary to give artificial respiration, use the mouth to nose method to avoid being affected by the poison yourself.

SPLINTERS Splinters are usually of wood and are generally quite easy to remove, with patience. Clean around the area, then sterilize a needle or pair of tweezers and try to ease or gently pull out the splinter, holding with the tweezers as close as possible to the skin. If it breaks or does not come out easily, cover the area with a patent softening cream (mainly beeswax) and cover for a day with a plaster. After this, most splinters come out very easily, almost on their own. There is no need to upset and possibly hurt a child by digging at the skin for long periods.

Where a splinter is large, dirty or deeply embedded, go to a hospital for attention. A tetanus injection may also be necessary.

SPRAINS AND STRAINS

Sprains happen when the ligaments round a joint are suddenly wrenched or torn, as when you turn your ankle while walking. Less serious than a dislocation or fracture, a sprain is nonetheless painful with swelling and, later, bruising.

Rest and immobilize the injured part, applying a cold compress to reduce swelling and relieve pain. Pad with cottonwool and bandage to support the joint and help keep the swelling down.

Seek medical advice. If in doubt about the injury, get the joint X-rayed in case it is a fracture.

Strain Here a muscle or group of muscles is pulled or overstretched so that it tears. It may happen while taking part in a demanding sport or exercise workout such as aerobics, especially if muscles have not been warmed up properly.

The sudden pain may be accompanied by stiffness and cramp; there may be swelling. Rest the injured part and apply a cold compress for half an hour. Pad with a thick layer of cottonwool and bandage to counteract swelling then rest the limb in a raised position. If you are worried that it is more than a strain, seek medical advice.

STINGS If the insect sting is left in the skin, remove with tweezers, taking hold of the sting as close to the skin as possible. Do not squeeze the sac at the end of the sting as this will force even more poison into the skin.

Relieve pain and swelling with a cold compress of sodium bicarbonate solution thoroughly soaked into a pad of cottonwool.

In the mouth Rinse the mouth out with a solution of one teaspoon of sodium bicarbonate to a glass of water. If the swelling causes difficulty in breathing, give the casualty ice cubes to suck and take to a doctor fast. Some people are allergic to stings and may react dramatically, even losing consciousness. Should this happen, put the casualty in the recovery position and get to a hospital quickly. Give artificial respiration if necessary (see pages 121-23).

STROKE With a stroke the brain is damaged by bleeding from a burst blood vessel or by the blockage of a blood vessel in the brain. The effects may be temporary or permanent, in severe cases causing loss of consciousness and paralysis, typically down one side of the body. A major stroke can be fatal but where only a small blood vessel is involved there can be a complete recovery.

The affected person may first develop a sudden severe headache, feel giddy and confused then, progressively, lose consciousness. Speech is often slurred and he may not be able to control his bowel or bladder.

All you can do is to try to minimize the effects of damage to the brain by keeping the patient breathing: loosen clothing and support in a half-sitting position with the head to one side so that any saliva can drain away. If he becomes unconscious, place him in the recovery position; if his breathing stops, clear the airway and give artificial respiration.

Arrange for urgent removal to hospital. Do not give anything to eat or drink.

As the right side of the brain controls the left side of the body and vice versa, so the effect on the body will be on the side opposite to the damage in the brain.

SUFFOCATION Suffocation is most common among babies and young children, often as a result of playing with plastic bags or having been sunk in soft pillows. Remove whatever is stopping the patient from breathing and comfort if distressed. If the patient is already unconscious, give artifical respiration (see pages 121-23) and call for an ambulance.

WINDING This may be caused by a severe blow to the upper abdomen (solar plexus) or a bad fall that takes the breath away temporarily. The casualty may double up with the pain and be unable to speak.

Let the patient rest comfortably until the pain passes and breathing is regular again. Complete recovery is the norm. If he is so badly affected as to become unconscious, open the airway and check breathing. Place in the recovery position (see page 124).

WOUNDS

Cuts, scratches and grazes Whenever the skin is broken there is a risk of infection from germs entering the wound, so always be careful about washing your hands before giving any first aid and never cough or breathe over a wound. Wash your hands immediately afterwards.

Stop bleeding by pressing a clean dressing over the wound (see Controlling blood loss, page 125), or round it if there is a foreign body in it that cannot easily be lifted out. To prevent knocking or catching such a foreign body, make a raised ring of padding round the wound with cotton-wool and put a bandage over until you can get to a hospital.

To treat the wound, wipe away dirt and clean the skin around it with a mild antiseptic solution, working always out from the wound. Then clean the wound itself with a fresh solution or under running water and dry with something clean and non-fluffy. Cover with a dry dressing, sterile if possible: an adhesive plaster is fine for small cuts but if the area is sore or raw use a bandage to hold the dressing in place.

Do not remove the dressing until the wound looks as if it is drying out and healing well, probably about a week.

If the wound is really dirty or deep, bleeds copiously or has jagged edges that might leave a scar, see a doctor. A tetanus injection and/or stitches may be necessary for such a wound.

Leg and arm wounds To slow down bleeding, raise a leg and let it rest on a chair (as long as no fracture is suspected). For an arm that is bleeding, hold in a raised position in a sling.

Puncture wounds Where a garden fork or a nail has gone in deep, there is a high risk of infection because of the dirt and germs that have probably been carried down into it, so take such wounds seriously even though they are small at the surface. A tetanus injection may be necessary.

TETANUS

Every wound carries some risk of tetanus infection but especially those that are deep or dirty or where there is tearing, from barbed wire or an animal's claws for instance. Immunization against tetanus should be renewed every five years.

TAKING THE PULSE

The pulse is the throb or surge of blood felt in an artery each time the heart beats. It can be felt where the artery is close to the surface of the body and can be pressed easily against a bone. The rate (how often per minute), the strength and the rhythm (regular or irregular) of the pulse act as indicators of the casualty's condition. Normal pulse rates are: adults 60 to 80 times per minute, children 90 to 100 times and babies 100 to 140 times but these may increase under stress.

To take the pulse at the wrist (radial artery), place the tips of the fingers on the inner wrist just below the thumb and press lightly. Do not use your thumb, as this has its own pulse.

The carotid pulse is taken at the neck in the hollow between the voice box and the adjoining muscle, just below the angle of the jaw.

In children, where the above pulses may be difficult to find, check the brachial pulse – on the upper inside arm, halfway between elbow and shoulder.

INDEX